A LETTER TO MY FATHER

WHAT YOUR SON WANTS TO TELL YOU BUT DOESN'T

ISAAC MOGILEVSKY

FriesenPress

Suite 300 - 990 Fort St
Victoria, BC, V8V 3K2
Canada

www.friesenpress.com

Copyright © 2019 by Isaac Mogilevsky
First Edition — 2019

All rights reserved.

No part of this publication may be reproduced in any form, or by any means, electronic or mechanical, including photocopying, recording, or any information browsing, storage, or retrieval system, without permission in writing from FriesenPress.

ISBN
978-1-5255-5234-2 (Hardcover)
978-1-5255-5235-9 (Paperback)
978-1-5255-5236-6 (eBook)

1. FAMILY & RELATIONSHIPS, PARENTING, FATHERHOOD

Distributed to the trade by The Ingram Book Company

To my mom, Debbie,
and my dad, Ian,
for your encouragement,
example, love,
and support.

Table of Contents

Letter 1: I Need You 1
Letter 2: Be Real 15
Letter 3: What Your Son Needs to Hear 27
Letter 4: Something Greater 41
Letter 5: I Don't Know What I'm Doing 53
Letter 6: What Matters? 67
Letter 7: Difference Maker 77
Letter 8: Wait for Me 87
Letter 9: Girls, Purity, and Waiting 99
Letter 10: Friend or Father? 113
Letter 11: Courage to Move 123
Letter 12: Looking for Success, Finding Wisdom . . 135
Letter 13: Where do we go from here? 145

Acknowledgements

If you were to tell me three years ago that one day, I would have written a book by the age of 20, I would have laughed at you. However, God has an amazing way of bringing me to places I never thought I'd be, through His power and through the help of the people that He places around me. I truly believe that this book would not have happened if it weren't for my family. My dad, for giving the initial idea for the book, going over rough drafts, making edits, encouraging, and showing the love of God to me throughout this process. His example of authenticity and vulnerability was essential in helping me approach this book in the same way. My mom, for being the best teacher anyone could ask for and for her unconditional love, support and encouragement even amidst of cancer treatments. Her perseverance and faithfulness to God even through hardship, kept me trusting God when I thought that this book may not happen. To each of my siblings, for their input, encouragement, and support throughout this project. My grandparents, for their unwavering love and support. To all of them, I am so grateful.

Also, I want to thank each one of the many friends and supporters who contributed financially to getting this book off the ground. Without your support, this book would not have been possible.

To my mentors and friends, thank you for walking with me through this journey and continuing to point me to Christ.

Introduction

Thousands of books have been written about the father-son relationship. For decades, books written by and for fathers on parenting have been flying off the bookstore shelves. Most of the customers are well-meaning fathers looking for helpful advice on how to build a relationship with their sons and affect them in a real, meaningful way. However, parenting books aren't the only medium that inspires fathers to be intentional about their relationship with their sons.

Maybe it was a men's conference that inspired you to get serious about developing a strong relationship with your son. Maybe it was an inspirational seminar about the great impact a father can have on his son's success. Perhaps, it was a thunderous sermon from the pulpit about God's design for the father to play an indispensable role in the life of his son. Whatever the cause, at some point you have sat down with your son, filled with strategies, methods, and concepts to share to help aid him and help him grow to become a godly man. However, to your surprise, it felt like the fatherly advice given was missing the mark, like it was disconnected from what your son really needed. You anticipated that this wouldn't be easy, and yet you believed with the right strategies and methods that you would be able to develop this deep bond and provide all that your son would need from you. Yet, it doesn't seem to be working. You want him to open up about his life so that you can apply all these great strategies and methods you learned in order to form a tight father-son bond, but you are left with a disinterested son. Feelings of inadequacy flood over you as a result of this seemingly helpless situation.

After other attempts to break through, you resort back to the good old pat on the back, capped off with a "you'll make it" or the even more comforting "you'll survive." Your heart breaks from the widening gap between you and your son. However, all you can seem to provide for your son is the occasional trite advice. You wish it wasn't this way; you truly want to pour yourself into your son's life and provide with him the tools that he needs to live a godly life, and further, to develop a strong relationship with him, but disconnection and disillusion seem to be the common outcome, regardless of what you offer.

The Gap

Today, the disconnection between fathers and sons is growing wider in our ever-changing society. Most sons give no indication outwardly that they really need their fathers, and give little indication of what they need emotionally or spiritually. Too many fathers see this as a license to step out of their son's life and take a backseat. As a result, sons are left to fend for themselves. Even though most of us see this gap widen between fathers and sons, both parties are often left confused as to how to break free from this reality and perhaps too complacent to try to find out what can breach this gap.

How do fathers reach through the gap to touch their son's lives and help them grow in godliness when their sons don't tell them what they need from them?

How do fathers make a real lasting impact on their sons in a monumental way if their sons don't communicate with them?

Maybe the better question is, do sons even want their fathers to be a major part of their lives in today's world?

The challenges facing fathers are more apparent than ever. Most fathers wish their sons would just spell it out, but they never do. As a result, most fathers are left in the dark as to what their sons need. For fathers who desire to have a strong relationship with their sons and guide them into a godly life, this experience is beyond frustrating. Fathers often look back at their own life and identify the things that they desired from their fathers and try to provide that to their sons. However, the world their sons are growing up in is different from the world in which they were raised. With social media, video games, cell phones, and many other things that are alien and have shifted from what fathers experienced growing up, well-meaning advice often goes unheard.

Is the answer to this disconnection to immerse yourself in current culture and learn all there is to know about your son's life in order that you can help him and connect with him?

Should you back off in hopes that he will come to you when he's ready to have you be a meaningful part of his life? Should you just be persistent regardless of the signals he's giving you?

These questions and more will be addressed here.

Brace for Impact

Few men, once they're grown, can say that their fathers have had no impact on their lives. Notice that I didn't say good impact. Regardless of what kind of father you had, fathers by design have the ability to affect their family, and specifically their sons. This was certainly the case for me and my father. So much of how I see the world and my purpose was formulated in conversations with my dad about living the Christian life. Growing up, you don't realize the magnitude of the influence and impact your father has on your life. Sure, when you're young, your parents are everything to you, but when you reach your teens, there seems to be a shift in how you view your parents—at least for most sons. It's ironic, then, that those are some of the most important years of adolescence. That's why the father-son relationship is tremendously important and should be taken seriously.

A Letter to My Father

This book is the beginning of a journey into your son's desires, hopes, dreams, wants, and needs. As a father, it is your opportunity to grow and step out of your comfort zone into what God wants to do through you. Moreover, it's a journey into learning to let the Spirit of God work through you as you minister to your son and connect with him in a real and authentic way.

You may ask, "How does this guy know what my son needs from me? How does he know that I can really help my son and encourage him?"

Take it from me: as a young man who has these issues fresh in his mind, your son does need you. You don't have all the tools to help him, you can't do it all, but if you begin on this journey of letting the Spirit of God work through you, the impact on your son's life will be immeasurable.

Looking back, there are so many things that I wish I would have asked my dad—questions that I had never asked, things that I desired of him that I never made known. But don't get me wrong: it's not a sad story for me and my father. We have a great relationship to this day. In fact, my dad's the one who encouraged me to write this book. However, there were things that were left unsaid, desires that were left unmet, and needs that were unfulfilled. This was not entirely the fault of my father, nor of mine. This is one of the main reasons that I am writing this book. As a young adult, I wish that had I told my father many things and made them known to him. This book, in a way, is that letter I never wrote.

Perhaps you would like to be a father someday. Maybe you have a son that's all grown now or maybe he's just a child. Perhaps you have a son that is in his teen years. Regardless, I believe this book to be an honest description of what your son wants to tell you, and what he desires of you. At the beginning of each chapter is a letter from a son to his father in which the son will express the many questions, doubts, and issues in his life. See the letters as a glimpse into the mind of your son, who has or will have the same questions, thoughts, and doubts. Sons, I hope that you will not only be able to relate to my experience, but that you will gain wisdom and insight from the lessons I have learned. Fathers, I hope this book will encourage and inspire you in this journey of connecting with your son in a real and authentic way. Remember that he needs you. He may not know it yet, but soon he will. God has you in his life for a reason. Don't waste it.

LETTER 1:
I Need You

Dear Dad.

I know it's been a long time since we've talked—I mean really talked—but I figured this would be the best way to finally walk on this journey together. I want to begin this by saying that I know I'm not the best at asking for help, or receiving guidance, or communicating with you about what really matters to me. I know it can seem like I want nothing to do with you, and sometimes, that's true. To be honest, sometimes I feel like I don't really need you that much. I know that sounds bad. But other times, I want to see if you'll stick with me. I want to see if you really want to be with me, if you're in it for the long haul. I know it won't be easy. Be patient with me; it feels like I have so many insecurities, fears, and questions that I don't know what to do with. It feels like I've been sent on a mission with no guide for how to accomplish it. I'm not sure what I'm asking, but I think I'm starting to realize I need you more than I thought. It sounds dumb, but I guess I'm saying I need you, Dad. I really need you.

Love,
Your Son

Most sons would rarely admit it, usually because of their tendency toward pride and self-sufficiency, but it's a fact: we need our fathers. As I grew up as a painfully sensitive child and then a teenager, I still had difficulty admitting that I actually needed my dad. Moving towards independence is such a highly esteemed value within adolescence, and I quickly learned that needing anyone, especially a parent, was socially discouraged. "Don't be a momma's boy" or "be your own man" were messages that I received from media that discouraged parental influence and involvement, especially fathers. Sure, it was great that my dad was there, but I believed early on that I had to make it through the challenges of young adulthood by myself. If I expressed my need for my dad, wouldn't that make me weak, needy, or dependent? Wasn't adolescence a time when I should figure things out on my own or with the help of my friends? I was wrong.

Carpool Conversations

Growing up, I loved sports, though not all of them sports. At the age of eleven, I was placed on a youth triathlon team—running, biking, and swimming. My dad and I would frequently make a forty-minute drive down to Birds Hill Park outside Winnipeg, where we would meet with the team to train. Living in a family of eight kids, this was one of the few extended periods that it was just me and my dad.

"How are you feeling about the race this weekend?"

I can remember my dad asking me this on a particularly warm Tuesday evening during our drive to the park. I didn't want to tell him how I really felt. If I were someone who loved triathlons, being a part of this team would have been ideal—but I didn't. In fact, I quickly realized that I wanted nothing to do with what felt like a normalized version of boot camp. How did I really feel about the race? I was terrified that I wouldn't perform well or I would fail, and anxious because I didn't want to let my dad down.

"Okay," I responded, hoping that that would be the end of the conversation. Dad seemed to be invested in the whole triathlon culture, so if I said how I really felt, I believed that I would be ruining the only thing we had together. Looking back, I'm amazed at the blatant lies that I believed about my relationship with my dad. I believed it was better not to open up to him to protect myself from disappointing him. I believed that what I felt was stupid and I should suck it up and not say anything to my dad about it.

"Are you excited?" he asked, trying to break through the obvious facade I was presenting him. That day, I told him the truth.

"No, not really. I don't think I'm any good at this stuff." This was true. I sucked at triathlons, but this wasn't the only thing that I wanted to get across to my dad. I was being honest, and I wanted to see how he would respond.

"Don't put so much pressure on yourself. It isn't that big a deal. Just try to have fun this weekend. Okay?" I nodded and inside I felt relief. It didn't matter how I did. My dad would still accept and love me. A lie was demolished in my mind and replaced with truth. My anxious heart was calmed by a few understanding words. After that weekend, I still didn't like triathlons and it wasn't long until I left the team, but I'm still thankful for being honest with my dad.

Those long drives out to the park were not the beginning of our relationship (that began at birth), but looking back at that time of my life, I was filled with fear and worry: Will I measure up to what people expect of me? Am I falling behind? Am I going to make it? These issues were magnified when I felt like I was battling them alone. It was the season of my life that I really knew I needed my dad. I would come to that realization many more times in my teens and young adult years. For me, it wasn't so much that I realized that I needed him for the first time, but that I wanted him to be an important part of my life. That response in the van was my first step into this journey. As I began to open up to him more, I began to desire his wisdom and input.

A Letter to My Father

What do you think?

Basketball camp—finally, something I could get on board with! At thirteen years old, I would be dropped at the University of Winnipeg bright and early on five consecutive weekday mornings in early July. Now rid of the days of triathlons, basketball was my sport of choice. After a morning of drills, games, and overpriced sports drinks, lunch was a coveted time of the day. During lunch hour on the second day of camp, I went over to a gathering of guys looking out a large window of the two-story building. They were jostling to get the best view, and I thought it must be spectacular. What I unknowingly walked into was a back and forth conversation about a girl, probably twenty years old, who was walking down below. As a spectator to the conversation, I grew increasingly confused and uncomfortable at the comments they were making about this girl's body. I knew it wasn't right, but I wasn't going to bring it up to my dad. However, when he asked how camp was that day, I knew I needed to tell him about it. Hearing from him that my confusion was normal really helped. Also, hearing that God's best for me was to respect women and not objectify them gave me direction. We talked for no more than fifteen minutes, but I didn't regret bringing it up to him. That was big.

All men have an innate desire to connect with their fathers and to let them have a lasting impact on them. However, this desire is often met with a number of lies that sons believe about themselves and their fathers. Disinterested fathers affirm these lies, such as "I'm not really worth his time." Our culture disregards fathers, which fosters lies in their sons' minds like, "My father doesn't understand me. He doesn't know what I'm going through. He doesn't care."

Sinful self-sufficiency that says only weak guys need their dad provides sons with an excuse to reject their father's guidance. All of these factors play into the suppression of a son's natural desire to connect and have his father lead him into manhood. When sons are confronted with the culture that tells them that their relationship with their father is not of great significance, and these same sons are met with a disinterested attitude from their fathers, this only reinforces the lies. Believe me, your son needs you, but he also hears a lot of lies telling him he shouldn't. Don't confirm these lies by your attitude or behavior; instead, affirm his desire for you to help and mentor him.

Obnoxiously self-sufficient

For some sons, it seems like they are totally self-sufficient from the time they hit adolescence. They can often present this false facade of self-sufficiency because they believe the lies that tell them they shouldn't need their dad. Often, when a father sees their son as self-sufficient, it affirms his false belief that his son doesn't need him and that he is unable to help him. Fathers, if your son comes across this way, don't be deceived. His confidence is just a facade that hides deep insecurities and longings. What we want to be striving for is to cultivate and foster a relationship with healthy independence, which your son will grow to cherish.

A Letter to My Father

Some sons have a unique way of acting obnoxiously self-sufficient as a teenager. It's their way of signaling to you that they are a man and that they are ready for what life will throw at them. Sons often put on a facade of what they believe to be manliness as a way to avoid rejection and hurt. You can't be rejected if you never depend on anyone, and you can't be hurt if you don't trust people to be there for you. This is just some of the thinking that contributes to this false facade of manliness.

I don't need to tell you that men have a hard time asking for help. Wait, let me rephrase that: men have a hard time even considering asking for help. There's a lie deep within the heart of a man that believes that if he needs someone else, that he is less of a man and a failure in some way. We all understand there would be a severe influx of families in their vehicles wondering foreign cities if it wasn't for wives "submissively" commanding their husbands to ask for directions. All that to say, your son is no different from you; he doesn't want to ask for help and guidance either.

How, then, do you reach out to your son if he doesn't want your advice and guidance, and perhaps doesn't seem to want to have a deep relationship with you? It's important that you have a base level understanding of his personality. Does he tend to be needy or does he like to act as independently as possible? Most likely, he's somewhere in between. This can help you find a starting place. I've already told you that your son needs you, and I hope that's beginning to set in, but knowing that isn't enough. You need to know what he needs from you.

Consistent Faithfulness

I was a needy and sensitive kid, which provided many difficult situations for my dad and me. Even as a teen, I carried that sensitivity into many different situations. I can think of one that felt like a matter of life or death: my driving test. I make light of it now, but at the time, that's what it felt like. Learning to drive was not a fun experience for me. I felt tremendous pressure at the responsibility of not running someone over. The time had come. I was either going to pass that test, get a great job, raise a family, and live a fruitful life, or I was going to fail and my life would be over. I know I sound dramatic right now, but it is amazing what a few lies can make you believe. I pulled out of the parking lot with the instructor and proceeded to cut off a truck that had moved into my lane (without signaling mind you, but I'm not bitter). I had failed. I was a failure. I was a disappointment. As I sat on my bed defeated, these lies took a hold of my soul. Just as isolation began to consume my thoughts, I looked up to see my father standing at the door. It took a bit for me to calm down, but his consistent presence was often enough for me to open up to him.

"We love you regardless, Isaac. Tons of people fail their first driver's test anyway. Is this all just because you failed the test? What are you really upset about?"

"Nothing, it doesn't matter," I lied. This was a phrase I found myself saying quite a bit in times of distress. "It does matter" was a response I heard and had anticipated, but I still wasn't quite ready to open up. "What if I fail the next one, and the one after that?"

My dad took a moment to gather his thoughts. "Being good or bad at driving does not characterize who you are or who God made you be. None of that is based on your driving skill." I believe that day to be the real beginning of my healing in this area of failure and how to deal with it.

What my father said changed based on the circumstance, but his presence was there regardless. His presence spoke so many more words of comfort and wisdom then he ever could. "It does matter" was verbal, but also sometimes a silent message I heard when my dad was there. This kind of faithful consistency is the beginning for a father on this journey to walk with his son. He didn't always know exactly what to say, but he was there. Fathers have a way of either distorting the character of God or rightly representing it to their son. In this case, he showed me that God was consistently faithful to be there in our time of need. Even when we feel like God isn't helping, we can have peace that he is always there; Emmanuel.

Worth My Time

Being there for your son is so important, but fathers nullify the beneficial results of consistent faithfulness if they unintentionally make their son feel like he's an inconvenience. Many sons already believe that of themselves, so don't affirm this lie. Being there is great, but your son wants you to want to be there—not just in times of crisis, but in times of normalcy and regularity too.

It's not about knowing about every little thing that your son needs from you and wants of you. We'll get into more of those areas later, but it is important that you are with him and that he knows that you want to be in this with him. He wants to know that he is worth your time. There are few things more damaging to a father-son relationship than when a son feels like his father doesn't want to be there.

If you are treating your son like he's worth your time, you are teaching him about the character of God. God is with us. He wants to be with us, but not because of how great we are; it's because of how loving and merciful He is. It's not like we as sons are just the greatest thing since sliced bread and God can't help but hang out with us. It is in His loving-kindness that He treats us like we're worth His time—even when we're not perfect. This same thinking applies to fathers: your son may be obnoxious, annoying, or rude, but it is through the Spirit of God that you can display a loving kindness towards him—even when he doesn't deserve it.

The Disinterested Son

One of the most discouraging and heartbreaking things that a father can be met with is a disinterested son. As a father, you've tried to be faithfully consistent in his life and yet it feels as though he wants little to do with you. Let's make a couple things clear: the fact that you have been there for him does not mean that he will be receptive to you, your wisdom, or your guidance. When this happens, fathers ask themselves, "Was I not there for him enough when he was young?" or, "Did I wrong him in some way that he still hasn't forgiven me for?" Maybe you did break his trust or wrong him in some way, which has caused him to pull away. There could be a myriad of reasons why he seems to be disinterested in having you be an impactful part of his life, but there is a better way than guessing.

I've talked a lot so far about being there for your son. However, I don't just want you to be there for him. I want you to make it a point to communicate with him and ask him questions. My dad had a way of asking us kids lots of questions. They represented more than the actual content of them because they told me that I was worth being known. Even when I was upset or angry, I would find myself opening up to him. He seemed genuinely curious about what was going on and how he could help. This kind of curiosity should permeate all your conversations with your son, regardless of the signals he's giving you to stay away. Instead of theorizing about why he seems disinterested in having a relationship with you, begin an ongoing conversation with him. Also, begin the process of reconciliation if you have hurt him in some way. Saying sorry first goes a long way.

Now I must warn you, this kind of communication can be extremely frustrating. Men, especially young men, have a way of shutting the door on conversations they don't want to have. They're great at shutting down when things get too real, but I encourage you to stick with it. Ask your son about things that matter to him, like hobbies, projects, and pastimes. Don't pretend to be into something you're not, but show him that he's worth knowing. The father-son relationship wouldn't be talked about so much if it was easy. He's not just a disinterested son; he's your son. Even when he acts that way, eventually he'll want you to be a part of his life. Give him time. I'll go more in depth on this issue in chapter 8.

You're Missing Out

I encourage you to continue on this journey. It's not easy, but it is worthwhile. Too many fathers miss out on the joy of making a significant positive impact on their son because they take a back seat when things get tough. I don't want that for you. That doesn't mean there aren't going to be problems, but it does mean that God knew what fathers and sons needed. As much as I've talked about sons needing their fathers, I could have equally talked about fathers needing their sons. Not in the same way, obviously, but God has designed the father-son relationship to be a sanctification ground for dads. It will give you numerous opportunities for spiritual growth. Patience, understanding, grace, loving-kindness, and courage will be needed on this journey as a father, and only God can be provided this through the Holy Spirit that leads to spiritual growth. Not only that, but the Spirit of God will work through you as you guide your son into a righteous and godly life, and God will grow you in the midst of that. Sons need fathers and fathers need sons—don't miss out.

This journey can have a generational impact when a father-son relationship is characterized by godliness. However, we are often caught up in the fantasies of what could be—what our relationships could look like, what are families could act like—and we act impatiently, expecting everything to change overnight. I would love to say that if you read this book carefully and apply all the tips, your son will suddenly act perfectly, accept all of your guidance, communicate with you, and have a strong relationship with you, but I can't. Your son will let you down, no question about it. I'm sure he already has. But you know what? So have you. You guys will continue to let each other down. However, by honestly working through disappointment with love and forgiveness, you can strengthen the bond between you and your son. One of the most impactful things my dad did for me was to point me to the heavenly Father, who would never let me down.

Show Me God

I mentioned earlier that a father has a powerful way of either distorting or displaying the character of God. Let me show you what I mean. As a father, you set the tone of your household. My dad did a good job at this, but I can remember one day, I was probably fourteen, when my dad had just gotten home from work. There had been a number of odd occurrences that day that had led to our house being more messy than usual. My dad began a conversation with my mom about the order the house was in. The conversation escalated after mom and dad left the kitchen. I remember thinking, "I can't believe Dad thinks this is Mom's fault. Why did he need to get so upset?" I felt like my dad was being unfair and selfish. I was angry at him, though I didn't show it. That was one of the few times in my life that I didn't want to be like my dad. The second story is that one day, my dad had just got home from work and he saw the floors filled with toys, the kitchen stack with dishes, and supper nowhere in sight. He got started, no questions asked. He made supper and got the kids to start doing their chores (which I had a hard time accomplishing). It wasn't just about the things he did, though, but the manner in which he did them. He wasn't doing these things begrudgingly, but because he honestly wanted to serve our family.

A father's actions and behavior is magnified because of their position of influence in the family. Don't take this responsibility lightly. You can show your son the glory of God based on how you live your life, but as I said before, you will fail at being the perfect reflection of God character. Instead, point your son to his perfect father, because your son needs you, but he needs Jesus infinitely more.

LETTER 2:
Be Real

Dear Dad,

It's me again. I figured if I stopped writing, you'd get worried, so here I am. It's tough for me to decide what to write to you about because there's so much going through my head right now. I guess I'll just start somewhere. Yesterday, I thought about how well you really know me, and for that matter, how well I really know you. To be honest, I wish you'd open up more to me. Sometimes I feel like I don't know you that well, and it's weird because I feel I should. You know? I barely know anything about when you were my age. What questions did you have? What doubts did you have? What experiences did you have that changed you? I guess I'm wondering, how am I supposed to open up about myself if I don't know who you really are? Some of my friends won't tell their dads much because they're scared they will be judged. I don't blame them. I've seen how their fathers don't seem to try to understanding them. I don't want that to be our relationship. I need you to help me through this, not judge me when I mess up or have questions or doubts. I want to trust you, Dad. Help me do that. I guess I'm asking you to be real with me. I know that's a lot to ask, but I'd much rather you be real with me than for us to keep closed off to one another. I need your help with this, Dad.

Love,
Your Son

Traveling with six kids (my oldest sister and older brother were not traveling with us at this point) was no easy feat. Long hours of driving, cramped quarters, and quick turnarounds from the hotel led to a difficult yet good family bonding experience. Growing up, I had a love-hate relationship with these trips. On one hand, I loved going to new places and eating fast food. On the other hand, the packing and unpacking, the crying kids in the van, and acting as a barf bag for my little sister led me to think this might not be my favorite thing in the world. You heard that right: my cute little three-year-old sister provided me with the great honor of being her barf target. In instances like these, you have to step back and laugh; however, I'm not sure my little sister will be laughing when she finds out I told this story here, but she owes me one.

A Letter to My Father

As a person who is embarrassed easily, road trips with my family were like kryptonite. It was inevitable that I was going to be embarrassed some time. Mostly, this was embarrassment for my family. Going into restaurants with little kids was asking to be uncomfortable for the whole meal. My dad was quite the opposite. He didn't avoid the embarrassment; he embraced it. He didn't care about what other people thought of our gaggling brigade. My dad was real; he wasn't trying to change his family into something we weren't. We were messy—not me, but my siblings. We were loud. Did people stare? Oh yeah, but that's who we were.

My dad wanted us kids to be real. I can remember on many occasions he would say, "Stop caring so much about what others think of you." He was right: I had a big problem of caring too much about what others thought of me. I cared so much that I put up a facade so people might like me more. I felt like they might not like who I was, so I showed them someone else. Not only did I care a lot about what others thought of me, I also cared a lot about what my dad thought of me. In fact, most sons do. We care about what our dad thinks of us. We want our fathers to like us, to be proud of who we are and who we're becoming. Some sons want this so badly, they present an alternate version of themselves to their father. Often, they do this for fear of being judged or rejected by him. This is just one of the issues that prevent fathers and sons from developing a close relationship.

It's a vulnerable thing to be real and authentic in this relationship because it exposes your son to the possibility of being rejected or judged. Often, it's easier to put a wall around us and not show our true authentic self to our fathers. These insecurities help foster lies in your son's mind like, "My dad won't like who I really am," or, "My dad definitely won't be proud of me," or, "My dad won't accept me." Lies like these prevent sons from opening up to their dads and being real with them.

Two Way Street

It always amazes me when I hear about a dad having trouble getting his son to open up to him, while on the other end, the father has no interest in being real and authentic about his own life with his son. It's a two-way street; fathers have to know that sons want them to make the first move. How do you expect your son to be real with you if you can't be real with your son? Both sides can be crippled with insecurities of inadequacy and rejection. They believe the lie that if they open up, they will be met with rejection or judgment. As a result, fathers and sons are often left at a standstill. As the father, it is essential that you make the first move, show your son who you are, and open up to him. He'll be glad you did. When your son feels like you trust him enough to be real with him, it allows trust to develop and sets the foundation for a real, authentic relationship. When he sees you trust him enough to be real with him, he'll want to do the same.

Accepted

I've mentioned before that I was a sensitive child and teen. Early on, I had no idea that was unusual and had no incentive to hide that aspect of who I was. Later, in my early to mid-teens, I came to an understanding based on what I heard from the culture around me that it was not "cool" to be a sensitive guy. None of my friends seemed to be like I was, and I felt like an outsider in this regard. As a result, I began to try to hide this aspect of who I was, not very well I might add, in hopes that I would not be seen as weird or "girly" to others. I put up a facade to avoid possible rejection. It was tough for me to open up to my dad about the things I was feeling or experiencing because I didn't want him to think that I was weak or overly emotional. However, when he began opening up to me, sharing with him was infinitely easier. We had a foundation of trust and I knew he accepted me. Because of that, I could be real with him. I wouldn't have to fear him rejecting or judging me. Relational authenticity could only take place when trust and acceptance were at the foundation. That's the key.

You see, I wanted acceptance from others, but I wasn't going to risk having them reject the real me, so I showed a counterfeit version of myself. Even if they still rejected me, they wouldn't really be rejecting me; they would just be rejecting a character I played. We all play a character to some degree, but when acceptance is at the base of a relationship, we can begin to break free.

Isaac Mogilevsky

Do You Smell That?

Growing up in a Christian home and being homeschooled, my parents taught me many things about God, the Bible, how to behave, how to think, and so on. Most parents have a similar role in their teen's life. Its importance can't be understated: pouring into your pre-teen or teen's life, fostering good character, teaching the truth—it's all important.

I want you to put yourself in your son's shoes for a minute. If you're a young guy, you'll know what I'm talking about. Picture for a second your father has just finished telling you that you don't need to be so worried about the future because God's in control. Perhaps you were fixated on what job you're going to have, what school you want to go to, or something similar. Your dad gives you this advice. It's good advice, right? Right. However, several hours later you come upon him and your mother having a heated argument about the finances that month. Do you smell that? Of course you do, and your son does too. You're not the only one who can smell a hypocrite, and your son's one of the best.

When fathers do or say one thing outside the home and the opposite inside the home, it tells their sons that their word cannot be trusted. They're sending the message to their sons that it's all a performance. Moreover, you learn that what's important is what you show to the public. As I said, sons are good at smelling hypocrisy. Don't think for a second that they'll take your advice if you don't take it yourself. Your son is looking for you to be real, not to put on a show. He is not looking for a perfect father who has it all together, but for someone who's real with him, who doesn't tell him one thing and do another, and who owns up to his mistakes. When you do this, you open the door for a real, authentic relationship, not based on a false facade but on transparency and trust.

The Tough Stuff

I was sixteen years old, sitting on our leather couch in the family room on a warm Sunday evening. We had just finished our family supper, which we had most Sunday nights. I was regretting the amount of food I had eaten as I watched a football game and a music award show in the commercials. I would occasionally turn on these types of award shows, but only to make fun of them—or at least that was my line. I actually liked that kind of pop music. Generally, I was good about changing the channel if something seemed inappropriate, but on this occasion, I may have let my guard down. A woman was doing a performance of a song that I particularly liked and despite her lack of modest clothing, I decided it was probably okay to watch at least part of it. My father occasionally glanced over to the television from the kitchen, where he was cleaning up from supper. He briefly saw what I was watching before I changed the channel. I didn't think too much of it, my guard was down.

The next morning, on our drive back from the gym, my dad wanted to talk to me about last night. "So, you were watching that award show last night?"

I didn't really know what he was getting at. "Yeah, it was pretty funny. Some of the performers just sucked." I expected my dad to joke about the skill of modern pop musicians, but I got something quite different.

"You know, you have to be careful with those shows. Lots of those women really don't dress that appropriately, you know?" There was a short of silence in the vehicle, then he chimed in again. "I just want you to be careful in what you decide to watch."

"Yeah, I know," I said.

Part of being real with your son is talking to him about the tough stuff. I don't just mean "the talk," but other tough things that we would prefer to leave unsaid. I know it must not have been the easiest thing for my dad to bring up, but he had to because he cared for me. It was more important for him to have an awkward conversation with me than for me not to understand the importance of the issue and provide guidance. The tough stuff doesn't just revolve around the guy-girl topics; however, I will go into more depth on this in chapter 9. This tough stuff could pertain to money, school, work, or friendships. Difficult conversations need to take place. Are you willing to have them?

Why is talking about the tough stuff so tough?

I like my dad as a person, not just a father, but I know that's not his goal. If that were the case, having those tough conversations would be impossible. Sometimes as fathers, you need to call out your son in a loving way, but this isn't always received well. You are often perceived as the bad guy in these situations. Nobody wants that. Often fathers are caught in the lie that their goal is to get their son to like them. Because of this, some fathers neglect to have tough conversations and be real with their son. As much as you may want your son to like you, that can't be your main goal. God has given you a higher calling in your son's life. You are called to have a real and authentic relationship with your son, where you can talk about the tough stuff and be real with one another based on a foundation of trust.

Your son isn't immune from the curse of sin. He will be wrong and he will behave wrongly. Don't just stand aside; have a tough conversation with him and help guide him. However, it's important to understand that these situations can't be handled rashly. Imagine if my dad had confronted me about the award show by saying, "Isaac, how could you watch that? I thought you were a Christian. Your mom's going to hear about this, and it won't be pretty." How would I have responded? Probably defensively. I would have shut down in a way. However, because my dad kept the door of communication open, we were able to be real and authentic within our relationship. In my mind, if my dad were to confront me harshly, why would I open up to him if all I got in return was his judgment? You see, it's a delicate thing to try to confront your son lovingly. That phrase sounds contradictory. To confront your son lovingly, it will lead to the mindset of concerned correction instead of judgment. Few things turn a son toward rebellion than the judgment of the father.

Your son doesn't need a judge, he needs a guide: someone that can take him aside tells him that he's wrong and to direct him toward a better path. Embrace the role of guide in your son's journey; it's much tougher than judging, but so much more fulfilling.

Share Your Story

Everyone has a story, events in life that have shaped them, principles that they have learned to live by, and wisdom gained through experiences and relationships. We live our story every day, with pages added and chapters finished. Our story is as personal as it gets. Our mistakes, our weaknesses, our hopes, our dreams, our failures, are all kept within the pages. Why don't we share our story? Is it fear of someone seeing our vulnerability, mistakes, failures, and all the stuff that we try to hide? Part of being real as a dad is about bringing your story into the light. Let him see who you are, who you were, and who you are trying to be. This kind of authenticity is perhaps the hardest to step into. You may ask that if your son sees your life for what it is—the struggles, the questions, the failures—won't he lose respect for you? No, quite the contrary. When sons see their fathers opening up in this way, we can see their courage amidst vulnerability, and it makes us respect our fathers more. Any person could hide their past—the highs and the lows and all the stuff that you would rather keep deep within the pages of your story tucked away on a shelf—but it shows us as sons your commitment to deepening the relationship when you tell it to us.

A Letter to My Father

However, I do have a word of caution as you share your story: temper your expectations of your son's response. When you open up to share aspects of your story, let it not be merely for the sake of transparency. If that were the case, you would need to share aspects of your past that do not serve any real benefit in your relationship with your son. Instead, approach these opportunities to be authentic as serving a greater purpose in the life of you and your sons as he begins to know and understand you, and as God begins to bring greater clarity to his story through your story.

Being real with your son is not easy. Fear can take hold of you, but God has called us to let our faith in Him overcome our fear. Fathers must have faith that through their authenticity, God will work in their own hearts and the hearts of their sons. Only when our lives are brought into the light can we began to develop real relationships built on trust. This kind of trust is built on honesty and truth—in speech and in action. Your son wants to see who you are, how you deal with situations, and how you act in the midst of difficulty. Don't hide that stuff. He wants to see who you are, and he wants to show you who he is. He needs you, the real you.

LETTER 3:
What Your Son Needs to Hear

Dear Dad,

It seems that writing these letters has become easier in some ways, yet I still seem to have a hard time picking up a pen. I guess it's tough to open up about some of this stuff, but here it goes. Sometimes I feel like what I'm doing is never enough. I know you love me, but it's hard for me to believe that when I feel like I haven't earned it. I guess I try to work harder to gain your approval, but sometimes it feels like you ignore my obvious attempts to please you. Do you even care? I want you to be proud of me, and I want you to tell me I'm on the right path. I want to hear that I'm okay—that I'm doing okay and that I'll be okay. Sometimes it's just nice to know that you're on my side, you know? I want to know that whatever happens, we'll still be in this together. I know that sounds corny, but I think I need that. I want you to be in this thing with me. Lately, I've felt like life is a roller coaster. There seems to be a lot of uncertainty in my life, and I need you to be on my team. I hope that makes sense. I like to hear from you and I wouldn't mind if it were little more often.

Love,
Your Son

Introspection is only beneficial for the individual when he or she is aware of their greater context. We all exist within a greater narrative. Our story is not left in isolation. When I was reflecting upon my own experiences as a younger teen, I tried to think of the things that I heard from my dad that affected me, or maybe the things that I might have wanted to hear him say. I always come back to three basic declarations from my father. The simplicity of these statements almost frustrated me. However, the depth to which they could be understood allowed me to be confident that they were more profound than I could have thought of on my own. They are: I love you. I'm proud of you. I'm on your side. These three statements can be said in seconds and yet they hold more weight than we usually attribute.

These statements have tremendous power. They can roll off the lips without a second thought. They can come from the depths of one's being to minister to another in a way that only could be possible with a transcendent God in our presence. We speak of the impact that fathers have on their sons, and yet we often neglect the mere simplicity of a couple of words. Your son wants to hear these statements; he needs to hear these statements. Let's explore.

I Love You

A theme in this chapter is that these statements are not merely impactful based on the words that are used, but on the conviction that the statements embody. Each of these statements embodies a greater set of sentiments that can play a key role in your son's life.

I love you. I heard these words so many times growing up and yet I didn't really know exactly what they meant. That isn't surprising, because we use the word love so broadly in our day. "I love this TV show." We use the word love to define many of our relationships with people and things. That's part of the reason I didn't know what my parents were trying to say when they said they loved me. I knew it was good, and even though I didn't know exactly what they meant yet, I was glad they said it.

When we are toddlers, our vocabulary grows tremendously and quick, but in order to understand the words we are trying to say, we need to see them in action. Wagon: show me a wagon. Carrot: show me a carrot. That's part of the reason that younger children are often caught talking about an immaterial concept as a material object. I don't know if you've ever heard a child do this, but it is one of the many amusing things that kids do at that age. "I want fun." Well, child, you need to know that I can't simply hand you some fun. It doesn't work that way. Even now, as we try to understand what love truly means, we want to say, "Love, show me what love is." Just as he wants to hear it, your son wants to see it. Then he can make the connection. When it's all words and no action, the power of our words becomes void and meaningless.

Manly Stuff

Guns, hunting, cars, fighting, sports, and the list goes on. The idea of manliness has been corrupted by our culture today. What we see as manly things can often be characterized as hobbies, and things that have been stigmatized are often necessary within the Christian walk. Let me explain.

God has created men to both give and receive love from people. This is all a part of how He wired us. He designed us to crave love from people and to show it to others as well. However, culture has distorted this desire. "Don't be emotional;" "Be a man, toughen up;" "Can we talk about something else?" Our culture wants to tell your son that he doesn't need your love, but that's not true. However, I often see dads playing into this lie by thinking that they don't really have any of these kinds of needs, so they ignore the "emotional stuff" because that's what men do, I guess. Why do we do this? Why do we ignore such an important part of our soul, the part that needs to both receive and give love? Do we think it's not manly? Is it too awkward to show love towards your son? Maybe so, but your son needs to hear from you, and he wants to feel the securing love of his father. I'll talk more about that aspect a bit later. For now, know that the culture lies to you about what your son needs. He needs to hear "I love you."

I'm Proud of You

"Look at me, Dad! Look at me, Mom!" When we were young, we wanted them to look at us, to see what we were doing. Why? Was our inner satisfaction of us doing something or accomplishing something not sufficient? Apparently not. We wanted them to look. Was our playdough sculpture really worth a second glance? Probably not, but that didn't stop us. This was the best we could do, all we could muster. A level of ignorance protected us from the crushing realization that what we created sucked. Those kinds of instances, regardless of the quality of work, are what I like to call "look at me moments." However, they didn't fade when adolescence arrived, though they did become more disguised. Perhaps they weren't as obvious as, "Look at me, Dad. Are you proud?" but they were there. Maybe they told you about something they did or accomplished, hoping for a proud response. That's a look at me moment.

Why do sons have these moments? Are they just bad at bragging or is there something else at work here?

From about the time of age thirteen to seventeen, I had a weekly routine of cleaning our whole house after everyone else went to bed, late on either Friday or Saturday night. I was an anxious teenager, like I said, and a clean house made me feel more at peace. As I was thinking about this odd routine, I was forced to dig deeper, because I knew there were other reasons for this. Cleaning the house wasn't just for me; it was for my family too. I loved seeing them respond to our house that was seemingly transformed overnight. It was my look at me moment. I wanted them to be proud.

We all have these look at me moments, especially as sons. We want our fathers to be proud of us, to affirm what we're doing or have done. The question is, as a father, when does your applause and commendations help foster an unhealthy pride in your son? It's an important question. As a father, you want to affirm and show your son that you are proud of him; however, you don't what him to have an unhealthy sense of pride in himself. First, understand that your son needs your affirmation in his life, no question. You're not keeping him humble by ignoring his successes or not commending his accomplishments. Second, your son doesn't need your applause with every little thing he does. He's not a child, but become aware of the moments when he's coming to you for affirmation. Be ready for those moments. In affirming him, you'll not be fostering unhealthy pride but grounded confidence. Could your son use this kind of affirmation to develop unhealthy pride? Yes. However, that is his heart issue that will not go away even if you stop encouraging him, so don't.

Get good at understanding when your son is having a look at me moment. That will help him develop confidence. However, that doesn't mean that you shouldn't give guidance and correction. On the contrary, he needs your affirmation, but he also needs you to correct him when he's off base. Encouragement and correction go hand in hand. This is the same correction and encouragement that God shows us as His children. God's support of us is not an avenue to be prideful, but rather to develop a grounded confidence in who He created us to be and who He is transforming us into.

Earn It

Perhaps one of the most important things to understand about your son's "look at me" moments is the tendency of some sons to try to earn and win over their father's approval. I can speak to this first hand. I have a natural tendency toward being a people pleaser. As a younger teen, I couldn't put it in such specific terms, but it was true. Tendencies like these usually bleed over into specific interpersonal relationships. I wanted people to be pleased with me, and more importantly, I wanted my dad to be pleased with me. I wanted to get his approval. I wanted to earn it. This was evident for me in the midst of the late-night cleaning, looking back on it now. I wanted my dad to be impressed. That's not a bad motivation, but I was approaching it as though I needed to earn his approval rather than a motivation to bless him through this action, because he's my dad. This is not a unique thing for sons; we want our fathers to be proud of us. However, some sons feel they are in bondage as they strive for their father's approval. You can help relieve them from this bondage by showing them that you are proud of them regardless of what they do. A couple of words go a long way: I'm proud of you. He wants to hear from you.

When we think of our relationship with God, often this same mentality applies. We want God to be proud of us; we want to earn his love and support. However, we can't earn his love; it is a gift, not something we can work for. I once heard street evangelist Tony Miano explain this idea this way: A young man walks up to one of his neighbors' doors and knocks on it. A middle age man opens the door and the young man asks him a question. "If I mow your lawn for you, can I be your son?" That's a rather odd question, but now think of a young man mowing his own fathers lawn out of love for his father. The son didn't try to mow the lawn to become his father's son. He mowed the lawn because he already was his son and the natural outflowing of that was showing love towards his father. I believe this to be a helpful example at how fathers ought to be interacting with their sons. You want your son to act out of a love for you and God based on the relationships that are existing, not working out of duty to try to appease your wishes. This is an important distinction and ought to be taken to heart.

I'm on Your Side

"Okay guys, new subs. We need Grant, Carter, Jake, Luke, and Isaac out there now. Comets on three. Ready? 3, 2, 1, Comets!" Community basketball—the rejects' league. Most of the guys on the team didn't make their high school team, but that made no difference to us. We were in the big leagues, or so we acted. We were twelve guys, all working towards the same goal. Regardless of how the game was going, we knew we were in this together. No one could act like he was somehow disconnected from the result of the game or season, win or lose.

Perhaps the greatest disruption to a team is when one member begins to act like he is separate from the team, or even to act as though he is on another team by down talking his own team or affirming other teams' accusations directed toward our team. When this happens, the team comes apart.

There is no doubt why so many people make a comparison of family and a team. It makes sense and the similarities are striking. This same comparison can be applied to the father-son relationship. Your son wants you to be on his team. He needs you to flourish. However, too often I see fathers acting like they're on another team in hopes that they propel their son to some kind of great success that their son hypothetically couldn't have reached if it weren't for their harsh criticism and condemnation. Your son is looking for people that can be in his corner. He needs people to be able to fall back on. When he's struck down by life, he wants someone to be on his side.

Think of a team again, what do teammates do for one another? They encourage, they challenge one another, they don't separate themselves when it gets tough - they get closer. These are all aspects of the teammate's relationship. I would argue that all of these issues relate similarly to the father-son relationship as well.

Encourage

Your son is growing quickly, and the opportunities, responsibilities, challenges, successes, and failures are coming at him faster than ever before. He's not sure if he can handle it, or if it's worth it. Success is amazing, but sometimes it feels out of reach. Meet him where he's at and encourage him. Help instill that grounded confidence in him.

When I was about seventeen, a friend encouraged me to start a blog. It was something that I never saw myself doing in a million years, but I did it. I wrote (and still write) articles about the Christian life and the challenges of being a teenage Christian. Early in my writing journey, the results of viewership didn't come easy. Discouragement sets in when you forget what your true motivation is. My mom and dad edited every one of my blog posts back then (and still do usually). I can remember one night when I was questioning whether or not I should keep putting out these blog posts consistently. Am I even good at writing? Nobody's even reading. What do I have to say that could be worth something to someone? I was insecure about my writing, about finding my voice, and about what people would think of me. My dad had finished reading the article when he looked up at me. "This is good, Isaac! I edited a bit here and there, but I really enjoyed it." Do you feel that? I certainly did. It was a sense of grounded confidence. "I can do this. I'm not wasting my time." I just needed him to tell me that it wasn't terrible and to encourage me to keep going. Your son needs that as much as I did. Met him where he's at and encourage him in what he's doing.

Challenge Him

"I don't know that I'm ready just yet." I didn't think I was prepared. What if I tried to take the next step in life and failed? It's much safer just to muddle around in life than to step out in faith in the face of possible disaster. It was late on Tuesday night, in the middle of my second semester at university. I had sat my parents down to try to convince them that I should drop out of university to pursue other life goals. This wasn't the first time I made this appeal, but it was perhaps the most pivotal meeting. I had just finished laying out my five-year plan. I was proposing to drop out of university, and yet postponing pursuing my ultimate goal (which did not include university) for the sake of more personal study and growth. I wanted to help people (still do), in a real meaningful way. I wanted to meet people where they were and help them see Christ in the midst of their struggle, but I didn't think I was ready. Lies tried to tell me that I should wait. I figured a good excuse was to say that I needed to study more outside of university, mature more, but excuses they were. I didn't know what it was going to look like. Would people want my help? Would I be able to help them? What if I couldn't make a career out of it? I figured I had better wait to study; it was safer. However, there was something I was running from. "Why not start now?" I was afraid this question was going to come up. "I don't know that I'm ready just yet." I was scared. What if I tried and failed? "If this is what you want to go for, then step out, stop making excuses."

My dad was challenging me like a good teammate. Like a good father. He was challenging me to look beyond myself, my insecurities, my fears, and look to Christ to use me. It was uncomfortable for both of us, and yet God used that conversation to move me into real action. Take opportunities to challenge your son and spur him into what God has called him to do.

Stick with Him... Even When it's Tough

When everything's going great for your son, sticking by his side, encouraging him, and challenging him will feel natural. However, when things don't seem to be going right and failure seems to be an ever-present reality, sticking with your son gets a lot harder. It's easy to start to step away when things aren't panning out, but he needs you on his side, regardless of how things are going. When you show him that you'll stick with him, a team mentality kicks in: We're in this thing together, no matter what.

We can see this as a characteristic of God. He will never leave us even when things get hard. He will never forsake us, even when we make a mistake. God is always present in the lives of His children. These same characteristics ought to be strived for by fathers. By doing so, you are not only being a good father, but you are giving your son an insightful understanding of how God treats his children.

I mentioned I went to university, but I can't say it was all cupcakes and rainbows. The first couple of weeks were overwhelming. It felt like every assignment was coming at me at once, syllabus after syllabus. I tried to meet my own expectations as well as the expectations I perceived my family having. A dark cloud made its home right above my head with no hope of removing it, at least not until

Christmas break. However, regardless of all the tough stuff I was dealing with, I saw my dad on my side. He was on my team. When I was frustrated with a grade, he reassured and affirmed my identity apart from school, and spurred me one to meaningful study. He was on my team through thick and thin.

I love hockey. Ever since the 2010 winter Olympics in Vancouver, I've been hooked. The intermission period interviews are always a staple of watching the NHL. However, I have a feeling that if you were to listen to them back to back, you could barely tell them apart. Perhaps the one phrase that is most common, even across other sports, is, "We just need to stick with the game plan." I can't tell you how many times I've heard this uttered by professional athletes. Why is it so important to stay with the game plan? The game plan keeps everyone on the same page. It gives the members of the team grounded confidence in what they are doing. When players stray away from the game plan, disorganization sets in. All of a sudden, this tense situation leads to frustration with each other and insecurity in the team as a whole.

Stick with the game plan. Encourage him, challenge him, and stick with him, even when things get tough. He needs you to be a good teammate, but more than that, he needs you to be a godly father.

What Your Son Needs to Hear

I love you. I'm proud of you. I'm on your side. You son wants to hear from you. He wants to see what love looks like. He wants to feel that his father is proud of him. He wants to know you're on his side. Tell him. Show him. God did not place you in his life to be quiet; He placed you there to tell him the things he needs to hear. Follow that call and speak.

LETTER 4:
Something Greater

Dear Dad,

Since my last letter, I've been thinking a lot about some different stuff. You know we're trying to be real with one another and I guess I still have a hard time talking to you about some things. I have some questions and I figured that you might have some answers. When I first became a Christian, it seemed easy, but lately I feel like it's an uphill battle I can't win. I want to live for Christ, but it's tough. What's the point? What are we trying to do? I feel like I'm trying to figure out all this stuff on my own, and it feels unfair because you been on this earth a lot longer than I have. You must have the answers, or at least some answers, but why don't you tell me? I know some of the answers to my questions may seem obvious, but sometimes spelling it out helps bring clarity to my mind. I'd rather hear it from you anyway. Help me to trust you enough to ask you questions, but even when I don't ask, please don't assume I have it figured out. Most of the time, I'm wrestling with something—either a question, struggle, or something else. I guess I'm asking you to help me make sense of all this.

Love,
Your Son

Brothers. They have the potential for so much good yet are sometimes the cause of pain within our lives. I have three of them and growing up was a mixed bag of good, bad, annoying, encouraging, and gross. I've shared a room with at least one of my brothers for the majority of my life.

It was a Saturday morning, and once again, our bedroom floor was a mess. Our family had repurposed an old storage room in the basement into a bedroom for my brother and me. We each picked a color to paint half of the room. Mine was a slightly darker baby blue and my brother chose a bright green. We were aspiring interior decorators; I could feel it. We had a wobbly bunk bed, but I guess that made it more exciting. It was great, or at least it was supposed to be. There was a problem though, and this was made evident on that Saturday morning in 2011. You see, my brother and I looked at managing a room very differently. My brother was all about practicality: if you use something a lot, leave it out. On the other hand,

I firmly believed that everything should be put away in its place regardless. I loved cleanliness; he loved practicality.

Because of this, on that Saturday morning, I once again initiated a conversation about the state of our room. Conversations like these certainly did not exclude personal jabs, insults, name-calling, and the like. It got ugly, and quick.

"Why is it so hard for you to just keep your clothes off the floor?" I asked my brother.

"I'll do it when I have time. Who cares if it's little messy?"

"I do!" I responded, thinking about resorting to harsher measures. There wasn't one bone in my body that could relate to his kind of thinking. He was crazy, or so I thought.

Although these altercations usually began with just the two of us, it wasn't long before one of us got Dad involved. I wanted things to go my way, for my expectations to be met about how the room should look. I felt like my brother was an obstacle to go through to get what I wanted. My dad was a means to get my brother to act the way I wanted him to, but Dad wasn't buying it.

"Dad, tell him he needs to stop being such a slob and lazy." It wasn't like I was interested in helping to better my brother, I only wanted to accomplish my goals. After things cooled down, as they usually would, my dad took some time with me. He asked me why I got so upset over something so small.

I disagreed with his premise. "This isn't a small issue, this is extremely important," I thought. Why was it so important to me? I couldn't necessarily put into words, but I know that it was and that was enough for me. This kind of perspective is not unique among younger guys. We have this limited view of what is actually important and what matters. I remember my mother telling me that a clean room wasn't more important than a good relationship with my siblings. I didn't believe her, nor my dad.

A Greater Calling

During my conflicts with my brother, my perspective was so limited, my desires so temporal, and my motives were self-centered. Part of the job as a dad is to point their sons toward a greater perspective. That's what my dad tried to do with me. "Isaac, try to be patient with your brother. You can't expect your room to be clean twenty-four seven. How do you think Jesus would want you to treat him?" Ah, this question, I had heard it before, and I knew the answer, but I didn't like it. I knew what Jesus wanted me to do, but what I wanted seemed most important. In the midst of this conflict, what I needed was to be called out of my limited perspective of what life was about. I believed life was about me, what I wanted. When things didn't go my way, I assumed they needed to be rectified. I could not for the life of me see that there was a greater calling in my life than this momentary satisfaction of having my room the way I wanted it. But my dad was trying to point me to something greater, to live for something greater, to live for Someone greater. I didn't buy in that day because I still wasn't ready. To live for something greater felt more like a jail sentence than a greater calling. To be patient with my brother and to forgive him even when he was annoying seemed like too much to ask of me.

Whether to live for something greater is really a question of whether to live out biblical manhood. When I was in conflict with my brother, I believed all that mattered was what I wanted, for my desires and expectations to be met. In doing that, I was suppressing the greater calling on my life, as we often do. We prefer to live for the present and avoid the hard stuff because we know this greater calling is a less comfortable calling. To ask me to forgive my brother was asking me to step toward a better way of living—a biblical way of living. However, it was also asking me to step into a less comfortable life.

How do fathers show their sons this greater perspective—God's perspective—and live out their Christian walk? Moreover, how do fathers inspire their sons to pursue a different way to live, counter to what the culture is telling them? The culture is telling your sons that it's about them. Self-centeredness is often passed off as good self-esteem and that responsibility should be avoided at all cost. These are just some of the issues that you need to combat as a father, as you seek to inspire your son toward something greater and biblical manhood.

Chores

Often, when we think of being inspired to do something new or live a different way, it excites us. Think of the times you've been inspired to do something or change the way you live. They were all things you were excited about. Why? Maybe you were inspired to take on a tough project and the possibility of success lead you to excitement for the future. Maybe the benefits of changing something about your life got you excited about making that change. Now think for a second. God has given your son a greater calling to live for God, to live out his faith, to live for something greater. However, this often isn't glamorous stuff. Thus, the thought of being inspired or excited to live out this greater calling is hard to come by. Let me explain.

Until I was about ten years old, I had only a couple of real chores. No big deal. I would spend the rest of what my family would call "chore time" touching up other people's chores to meet my desired specifications. I know this may sound weird to you. I was an odd person, and still am. It was great. I didn't have to do it if I didn't want to, but I was able to get the house looking like I wanted. However, it all came apart on one fateful day after I had turned eleven. My older brother and sister had schemed to get me on the chore roster, and they were successful. It didn't take long for me to realize that having responsibilities was tough and that it was much less fun than being a freelance clean freak, but it was a call into something greater. I felt like I was needed, and that my work was important to the family. I don't think I'm exaggerating the occasion of an eleven-year-old doing chores, but it was the tangible beginning of my journey into manhood and a greater calling.

In Their Sights

Sons watch their dads, maybe even closer than their dads would like. However, this reality is your jumping off point as you try to inspire your son to live out his faith while you live out yours. Do you wish your son was excited about living for something greater? Show your son your excitement. Do you want your son to be inspired to embrace God's call of biblical manhood on his life? You first get inspired to do the same. Don't get me wrong, I'm not saying these things are totally contingent on you being the perfect example, I talked about that in the last chapter. It's about letting your son thrive off your contagious inspiration and excitement to live for something greater. As a kid, I remember my dad serving dinner. He often made supper on Sunday nights and was excited to serve his family. Remember earlier in the book when I talked about how fathers have the ability to show God's character to their kids? This was another of those instances that he not only showed me God's nature of servanthood, but he created an environment of stepping out into something greater, to serve and place others' needs before my own. It wasn't a particularly manly task, but in serving, he was showing me what it looked like to be a man following God passionately.

Your son sees you. He hears what you are saying, but your actions and attitude also play a key role in your model living out this greater calling that God has for you.

What does following a greater calling look like?

I've told you that you can inspire your son toward this greater calling through your example, but what does that look like? There are many calls given in the Bible towards men, some of which I will be covering in this book, but there are a couple things I want to emphasize here about following God's greater calling.

The biggest thing we need to understand about following God's calling into something greater is that it requires us to lay down our own will. This is essential to understand as we begin to step out into God's call on our lives. In the last chapter, I emphasized being real with yourself, in your relationships, and with God. This takes stepping out of your comfort and safety of being closed off and moving into the vulnerability of authenticity. You must lay down your pride to be real. You must lay down your desires of what to manufacture your son's perspective of you. This is all for the cause of following God's call into something greater.

Likewise, being a servant takes stepping out of our own desires and expectations and asks us to move into what God would want for us. Following the call into something greater takes stepping out of our insecurities, selfishness, lies we believe, all the things that are keeping us from this better way to live, and embracing a real authentic, inspired, and passionate lifestyle of following His ways.

Why live for something greater?

We can imagine what it looks like to follow this greater calling, but why should we live for something greater? Do you have an answer? You son is going to be coming for an answer, eventually. He'll want to know what life is all about. However, he usually won't ask directly, so get used to that. Sons are good at asking you subliminal questions without asking you a question. When they were small, they'd ask questions all the time. For many kids, their favorite question is 'why?' Why is this the way it is? Why should I be nice to my sister? Why do I need to go to bed? As a kid, questions are easy to ask. When a boy gets older, asking their dad a meaningful question is hard to do. Remember that. Just like it's sometimes hard for you to engage your son in a meaningful conversation, it's also hard for your son to ask you questions. But the more he trusts you, that you won't reject or judge him, the more he'll want to ask those tough questions. Take it from me. Because few sons ask these questions directly, sons rarely hear why they should live for Jesus, they just hear that they should.

What's the point?

The cool morning air blew along our street as the sun made its presence known with an occasional blinding glare. My iPod read 7:30 am as I drank from my leaking water bottle. Swish, swish, swish. The sound of the basketball going through the hop was pleasing yet became unsatisfying fifteen minutes into my morning practice. I was fifteen years old, and now they grouped us with boys all the way to eighteen years old. It was a big year. It was partially what led to this less than common morning practice.

As I practiced, I considered a question that often came to my head as I was experiencing a higher level of weariness than usual: What's the point? As I said, this was not the first time I had asked myself this question. In fact, it came up often. It wasn't just asking for a philosophical take on sports and competition; I was asking what's the point of everything. "What am I doing here?" We all have these questions, and we must look outside of ourselves for answers. Sons are looking for the answers. Can you tell him the answer? Do you know the answer? Most likely, you've wrestled with these questions at different points of your life, and because of this, you have an amazing opportunity to bring that wisdom to your son. Perhaps he won't admit he's having these kinds of questions, but at some point, he's going to be asking them himself, and he's going to be looking for answers. Too often fathers are capable disciplinarians, form good character in their sons and set good moral standards, and yet rarely put these things into proper context. Why have good character? Why follow this greater calling?

Your character is important. That is one of the main points of this chapter, but it is also extremely important to tell your son why having a godly character is important.

For many years, the concept of doing good and the message of Jesus dying on the cross were disconnected. I heard my parents talk a lot about good character and behaving well, and I also heard about Jesus dying on the cross, but I didn't understand how they connected. I was confused about it but would never think to ask a question. This disconnection was not the fault of what I was being taught, but just as a result of my young mind not putting the puzzle pieces together. This disconnection was very present in my life until I was listening to a podcast one day, and it clicked. It really clicked. They didn't say anything I hadn't heard, but I heard my answer. What's the point? Why follow Jesus' calling into something greater? Because Jesus died to take the penalty for my sins so that I could be forgiven. Moreover, it was so I could now live free from this bondage of sin and pursue God's greater calling on my life to live as a disciple of His. I'd heard it before, but it just took going back to the basics to make it click for me.

Maybe your son has it all figured out, but I doubt it. Most likely, he's asking the same questions I asked. He's trying to figure out why this greater calling looks like. He wants to see it modeled. He wants to know what the point of all this is. Can you tell him? Godly character is so important, and much of the rest of this book will be spent talking about it, but if all you tell your son to do is to live more as Jesus lived, and rarely tell them why then you're missing the point. Tell him why and then call him into something greater. That is how our journey continues.

LETTER 5:
I Don't Know What I'm Doing

Dear Dad,

To be honest, I'm just confused. I feel like my life is a ticking time bomb and I need to make the right decision about which wire to cut to disarm it, but if I make the wrong decision, it's going to blow up in my face. I feel like everyone around me already knows what they are going to do with their life. They already know what their life is all about. They have a five-year, heck, some have ten-year plans, but I feel lost. There seem to be so many factors that I need to take into account. Should I go for something predictable, stable, and comfortable, or should I take a chance? Maybe I should pursue something risky, something exciting, something strange. Want does God want me to do? Right now, I have no idea. What do you think I should do? What if I make the wrong choice? What if I cut the wrong wire? I don't know, I'm just scared. I wish I could just see five years ahead in my life. That would clear things up. I could see everything I need to do to get exactly where I'm supposed to be. But I guess it doesn't work that way. I guess we wouldn't need to trust God if we could see the future. I know that was a lot, but all that to say, I could use your help on this one. I act like I've figured it all out, but that's only to cover up my insecurities of feeling like I don't know what I'm doing. Can you help?

> Love,
> Your Son

Purpose. What's mine? What should I do with my life? What could I do with my life? Sons ask themselves questions but they are rarely given the proper attention.

We live fast-paced lives with no time to think, take a step back, or examine. But your son is getting closer to entering this race. He wants to know what he's going to be doing and why he's going to be doing it. We all have these questions. Some are confronted with them early in their lives but push them deeper into their unconscious. Others have these questions, ask others for the answers, yet are handed answers that are so light they float away. These answers don't hold any weight and leave a longing soul still on the hunt. Depending on the age of your son, he may not be able to put it in such terms, but there is a pull in all of us to have a reason. What is my purpose? This is the question we would all like to have answered. First, let's look at a simpler time.

Looking back at myself growing up, I had many dreams and aspirations of what I wanted to do with my life. As cliché as it was, one of my first dreams was to become a firefighter and policeman. However, I was hoping that being a policeman would be similar to playing cops and robbers, except with real guns. It didn't take me long to realize that that wasn't the case, so I moved on to another dream: to be an astronomer. I had received a book on astronomy for school and I was mesmerized. Studying planets and stars seemed to be a job with no drawbacks. I remember telling one of my friends about my newfound love for intergalactic research. He asked me if this was another one of those dreams that I would ditch in a couple weeks. I told him it wasn't—but it was.

When I was about twelve, I took acting classes regularly and I was in musical theatre as well. I was going to be an actor. I really felt I was good at it. Everyone else was too quiet on stage, but I was not afraid to put myself out there. If you were to ask me if I thought of myself as the next Leonardo DiCaprio, I would have stared at you blankly because I wouldn't have known who you were talking about. To me, the story of the Titanic was still about all the people dying and less about the actors and fictional characters that I had never heard of. Regardless of my lack of current celebrity insight, I knew this was where I was meant to be. This was my destiny. Okay, maybe not. A year later I moved on to something else. I guess I was a serial dreamer.

As I got older, the concept of finding purpose in my life got even more real. What do I do with my life? What does God want me to do with my life? What am I here to do?

Something I discovered early on in my life about myself is that I want a reason for what I'm doing. I need a goal to accomplish, an achievement to reach. However, the search for purpose and meaning is often met with a myriad of reasons for doing other things. Let me explain.

Sons hear so many things from the culture about what we should do with our lives. "Do what makes you happy." What if playing video games make me happy? "Follow your heart." What if my heart doesn't know what I should do? We want to know what we should do, what our life should be about, but the answers we get don't make a lot of sense. I want you to help your son find his purpose, but to do that, you need to have a clear idea of what purpose means. What is our ultimate purpose? Where do we find purpose in a general sense? That's what I call general purpose. Where can we find purpose in a specific sense? That's what I call specific purpose. How is ultimate purpose related to general and specific purpose? These distinctions are crucial in our understanding of our purpose on this earth.

Ultimate Purpose

What am I here to do? What is my ultimate purpose? Image God. Plain and simple. But what does that mean?

God created us in His image. Further, He created us to image or reflect His character, His goodness, His mercy, and His creativity to all creation. In that, God would receive glory. We were made to tell God's story, to show who He is through who we are as new creations in Christ. Our ultimate purpose is to glorify God through our lives. We are to show the world what God is like through the way we live our lives. Moreover, to show God's transforming power in the way that he changed us from lovers of self to lovers of God. All humans have this ultimate purpose placed on their lives.

What do we do with this? I'm supposed to image God on this earth, but practically, in what context am I supposed to do that? It is essential that we understand our ultimate purpose, but once you understand it, what's next? The answer is that of our *general purpose*, which is informed by our ultimate purpose. I'll explain.

General Purpose

When I talk about general purpose for sons, usually it is related to career, occupation, life goals, and things like that. We want to know what career to pursue. We want to know what life goals we should strive after.

Nearing the end of my years as a high schooler, it was becoming more apparent that my decision of what I was going to do next was imminent. How is an eighteen-year-old supposed to know what he wants to do for the rest of his life? I asked this question many times. It didn't make sense. How was I supposed to know what kind of job I wanted to do for the next forty-five years? Eventually, I landed on engineering. I was pretty good at math and I did calculus in high school. Okay, I can make this work, I thought. But I was scared. What if this isn't what I'm supposed to do? Like I said before, our ultimate purpose will inform our general purpose. In clearer terms, that means that what job I pursue should be one that I can do as I fulfill my ultimate purpose of imaging God. That leaves most jobs as an option, with a couple of exception. Did being an engineer meet those criteria? For sure. Did that mean I was meant to be one? Not necessarily. Other factors played into it. What am I good at? What do I love to do? Do I like to work with and help people? What's my personality type? These are all good questions to answer with your son as you explore this aspect of his general purpose. Another aspect of general purpose may be choosing to be married and have a family. That can also be a huge part of your son's general purpose depending on what stage of life he is in. I will talk more about that in a later chapter. All those things are aspects of your general purpose.

Specific Purpose

What do I do right now? The answers to that question is what I call your specific purpose. But how do you know the answer to that question? And further, how do you help your son answer that question? Remember your ultimate purpose; glorify God and image Him on this earth. Now you ask the question, "What do I do right now?". Well, similar to your general purpose, you must let both your ultimate purpose inform your specific purpose. This line of thinking ought to seem fairly logical. This is really important if your son is a logical thinker. He'll want to know how this all lines up. Regardless, use this three-tiered model of purpose to help your son discover his.

The question of what you should be doing can be overwhelming. You can think of all the possibilities of things you could be doing right now, even the things that align with your ultimate purpose, but the list would be huge! As your son approaches his mid to late teens, this search for purpose will move to the forefront. Now, it is important to acknowledge different perspectives on this as well as the importance of life circumstance. First, I want to be clear that your job will never satisfy the longings of your soul for a true purpose. Only Christ can begin to give us this kind of satisfaction by His grace, but even then, it won't be full or complete until heaven. So, if you are encouraging your son that he can find his kind of purpose in a job or career, you're leading him down a road with inevitable disappointment ahead. We were created to work and find meaning a purpose in it, but it was not meant to fill the central longing in our soul for purpose and meaning. Only Christ can fill those aspects of ourselves.

Nevertheless, we still need to work, take on meaningful responsibility, and live our lives with tangible purpose. Because of this, I believe it is valuable for you to walk through this area with your son.

What's My Purpose?

So much of the worry and anxiety around young men finding their purpose is that they believe that they only have one purpose throughout their whole life. That is true concerning our ultimate purpose; however, that is distinctly false regarding our specific purpose. Even with aspects of our general purpose like a career, many people change their direction through their lifetime. Our general and specific purposes are influenced by our context and stage of life.

The idea of finding our purpose is often a scary thing for young men, simply because we put so much pressure on finding our one true life-fulfilling destiny. We feel that once we find it, our life will make sense, we'll have perfect direction, immense fulfillment, and an ultimate contentment. Your son needs to hear from you that it doesn't work that way. Over a lifetime, we will have many different things that God has called us to do that are our purpose in that specific time in our lives or for a season. However, when young men hear the world's message that they need to find their one true purpose to be satisfied, this seems overwhelming, and rightfully so. Fathers can play a great role in this story. A father needs to understand what his son is going through and help bring some confidence, clarity, and calmness to what seems like an overwhelming situation. You can begin to do this by helping your son get a clear vision of his ultimate purpose. Through that, you can help him hone in on his general and specific purpose.

Your son has many questions, and explaining this stuff to him can help him find answers.

Do I have to?

Responsibility. What was your response to reading that word? Excitement? Inspiration? Meaning? Purpose? I would guess for the vast majority, it's not.

Why is that? Why do we have such a visceral reaction to responsibility? We dislike responsibility and the pressure that comes with it. Responsibilities are not easy, and ever since the fall of Man, we've tended toward and desired ease and comfort. However, the problem is that the things that we tend to avoid, such as responsibility, are the very things that bring purpose and meaning to these aspects of our lives.

Perhaps your son has figured that out, he is smarter than I am, because it took me quite a while to understand this fact. If he is like I was, then he's going to need some help.

Young men don't just wake up one day and figure out that what's missing from their life is more responsibility. As I said, it's Man's fallen nature to avoid responsibility, but that responsibility will help bring purpose to these aspects of their lives. As much as young men try to avoid it, responsibility is an aspect of all our lives. You can either thrive on it, derive purpose from it, or you can whine and complain about it. So much of our culture nowadays consists of young people looking endlessly for meaning and purpose apart from God's design for us. Instead, they're told to follow their passions. It's not bad advice, but it comes with additional advice that tells them to follow only their passions that are a void of responsibility and consists of pleasure and momentary excitement. However, what we are seeing from many of these young people is that because they follow these passions that are devoid of responsibility, they are left void of purpose and meaning in their lives. This is no surprise to God. He designed it this way. He wanted men to embrace responsibility, to embrace their duty as His image bearers (women likewise have this duty), and find real purpose.

Your son is looking answers. Use responsibility as a springboard. Counter the lies that he's hearing from the culture about the scourge of responsibility on our culture. However, I want to give you a warning: if you're telling your son about the wonders of responsibility and the great purpose that can be derived from it, and yet he sees you agonize over your own responsibilities, he won't buy in.

Why should he? If his own father seems to have the same visceral response to responsibilities that he himself has, he must be getting something right. But he's wrong, and you are too if you have that visceral reaction to responsibility. Look, responsibility is not always fun, but having a purpose is better than having fun. No question about it. In fact, responsibilities can lead to some of the most joyous occasions, but it will also reap some of the most difficult ones.

Your son needs to hear that we move towards living a purposeful life for God, because that is where our souls can get a taste of what our ultimate fulfillment will be in Jesus. Responsibility is not a symptom of the Fall, but our response to it is. Help your son fight back against this fallen tendency to dislike responsibility. Through it, you both may begin to experience a glimpse of your ultimate fulfillment in God.

The Money Problem

I want to go back and finish telling the story about how I wanted to become an engineer. As I said, it was getting close to high school graduation and I needed a direction. My criteria for choosing a career were not unusually stringent, but there were a couple of things that mattered to me in a job. Number one, I wanted to be good at it. Like I told you earlier, I was pretty good at math. Number two, I didn't want to be in university forever, so the program length would have to be limited. The programs I was looking at were 4-5 years, and I could handle that. Number three, I had to make a lot of money. I wanted to make a six-figure salary one day. Why? It may not be for the reason you think. I wanted to get married one day and have a family, so I figured if I made a lot of money, it would be a lot easier to make everything work.

The problem was that I let this idea of making six figures close off many jobs that I actually wanted to do. Being an engineer sounded cool, but upon further investigation, I knew it wasn't for me. I was at a crossroads. Should I pursue something that I knew I wouldn't enjoy but be wealthier, or pursue something that I loved and what I thought God had called me to and leave my finances in His hands? This is where I was. I ended up choosing the latter. However, I don't want to give you the wrong idea. God very well might call your son into a high paying job. If so, that's great, but if He's not, don't let the money get in the way of you encouraging your son into what God has called him to do. I know it's scary. What if he won't be able to provide for himself or his future family? What if he changes his mind too late? It would be a lot easier for fathers if every son just became a doctor, engineer, or lawyer, but many will not. Your son may not have a straightforward career—it may be risky; it might be a little crazy—but the last thing a son needs from his father is a blanket 'no.' Talk with him. Guide him. He doesn't have a lot of stuff figured out yet and telling him no without authentic communication just sends him back to square one. Why is it a bad move? Is it really a bad decision, or is your fear for your son's future getting in the way of you encouraging him into what God has for his life? Your son is fighting that fear too; the fear is even stronger for him. As I talked about in the last chapter, this is his call into something greater. Walk with him in it. If your son does get a comfortable, stable job, that's great, but be careful to not let worldly determinants like the love of money or security be the deciding factors.

What now?

After deciding that I didn't want to be an engineer, I decided to go to university for one year to see what was up. After that, I decided it was time to take my blog to the next step and do what I believe God had called me to do. A couple months later, I started Daily Disciple, a ministry dedicated to helping people become authentic, inspired, and passionate disciples of Christ. I was writing blog posts, making videos, and helping people online and in person in their walk with Christ. For now, I knew what my purpose was and I cast fear aside and trusted God. This is what He has called me into. However, I wouldn't have followed this purpose if it weren't for my dad's unwavering faith that God would work it out. When I felt like my dad wasn't worried about the money or how everything would work out, it gave me license to trust God. I had my purpose. Encourage your son to follow what God has for him today, to glorify Him, regardless of his fears, insecurities, or worries. Also, show that to your son. He'll thank God that you did.

LETTER 6:
What Matters?

Dear Dad,

I hope I'm not overwhelming you with all these letters, but at the same time, I'm overwhelmed. There are so many things racing through my head right now and it's hard to step back and take a breath. I guess I want to know where I should put my energy and my passion, you know? I feel like there are so many things that I could care about, but I just want to know what really matters. More than that, I want to be passionate about what God is passionate about, but I'm not sure what that looks like. I don't even know the first step to do that. How do I use my passion for God? I just want to know, but at the same time, I feel myself sometimes putting my passion toward things other than God. I guess I'm asking for some help and guidance. I hope that's not too much to ask. I just don't know who else I would go to. I'll write again soon.

> Love,
> Your son

"Okay guys, I'll see you Sunday at the Lindenwoods Community Center. Be ready for the game and let's play well!" As sweat dripped down my face, I reached to grab a towel from my gym bag. I had started a trend within my basketball team to bring a towel to games and practices. The truth is, I only started bringing the towel because my hands got really sweaty when I was nervous. Playing basketball, I was frequently nervous. Because of this, my hands would get sweaty early into the game. This was a real nuisance on a couple of occasions when the ball would slip out of my hands, to my embarrassment. Regardless, all the guys on my team started to bring towels. I was a trendsetter.

That day I had a mission. After practice, I was going to share the gospel with one of my teammates. I had been listening to a podcast about evangelism for quite a while beforehand, and I was ready to put what I heard and learned into action.

My hands were sweating out of control and my heart was beating out of my chest. I couldn't breathe. I had set up a mental game plan that consisted of me beginning a conversation with my teammate Ryan. I would then shift the conversation to Jesus, hopefully smoothly.

Ryan, providentially, lived close to me and we took a similar route home, which would be my opportunity to

A Letter to My Father

tell him about Jesus. I picked up my bag and hurried out the gym door, where Ryan was taking with some of the other guys.

After they finished, we walked along the sidewalk. I was trying to build up the courage to bring the conversation to a spiritual focus, but he changed the topic first. He asked me if I went to church. I couldn't believe it; this was it. God had thrown me the alley-oop and I was about to finish with a slam dunk. I said yes to his question and preceded to ask him a question as well. "Do you believe in God?" My voice quivered.

"Not really," he responded, adjusting his hat with his long curly hair spilling out the sides.

I didn't know what to say, so I took a breath and asked another question. "Are you an Apheist?" No, that was not a typo. That's what I thought the word was. Did my teammate know my mistake? I don't think so; he was just as clueless. Regardless of the lack of proper understanding of terms, I was able to share the gospel with Ryan that day. My first witnessing experience didn't go perfectly, but it's fun to laugh about it now. I was passionate, I was young, I didn't know a lot of things, I had questions, but I wanted to see people come to Jesus.

When I think about the passion of a young person, two things come to my mind. First is the great excitement, hope, and joy that can come from being passionate about something that matters to them. Second is the ignorance, impulsivity, and destruction from unguided passion. These two outcomes are very real realities in the lives of young men.

What matters?

What makes life interesting? Mere apathy towards life? Of course not. We want to care about things. We want to be passionate about issues. We want to put energy into what matters to us. We can see this is evident throughout our culture. Whether it is in sports, politics, celebrities, movies, theology, we like to get passionate about a cause. However, to get passionate about something, we need to have some explanation as to why this is important. For example, if your son has ever been passionate about a videogame and perhaps is in the market for the newest game release, he may begin to pull out all stops when it comes to convincing you why it matters. He might say, "Listen, Dad, it helps with logical thinking, problem-solving, hand-eye coordination, and it's exercise!" The last one always makes me laugh when I hear it from my brothers. Waving around a remote is not my definition of exercise, but I skipped the jog I was supposed to go on this morning, so who am I to judge?

I'm not trying to trash talk videogames. We like to be passionate and we usually have an explanation for why what we're passionate about matters. We were designed this way, to get excited and passionate about things that matter. However, there seems to be an epidemic of disappointed Christian dads, because they see their sons so passionate about things that they don't think matter. Videogames, sports, social media—you would be hard pressed to find a young man who wasn't overly passionate about one of these things in your neighborhood. It's important to understand where your son is coming from.

A Letter to My Father

It is not beneficial in any regard to insult or criticize the thing that matters to him. Instead, it is your job to help redirect him and utilize aspects of what he already cares about towards fostering good, productive, and godly passions.

Your son needs to know that we all have unique areas that matter to us, but we all should be striving to live for God while considering our unique passions. Our passion for God should engulf our other passions. That doesn't mean that our other passions disappear, but it does mean that there are redirected into something greater.

Here's an example. Say your son loves videogames. You see his passion and it seems misguided to you. Take a second to think. Instead of criticizing his choice of passion, inquire further. Conflict and broken relationships materialize when assumptions are made about your son's motivations. What does he like about videogames? Do you know? Maybe it's the storytelling. Maybe it's the art. Once again, think: do those things matter? Do art and story matter? They do. They reflect God's creativity and order, and that matters.

You may still have a hard time understanding your son's love for videogames, but upon this deep reflection, you understand the redemptive qualities he is drawn to. Cling to those and help your son foster this passion for story and art. It may not be your thing, and that's okay. You son's not asking you to know all the intricacies of his passion, but he wants you to at least try to understand.

How You Play the Game

"It's not whether you win or lose, it's how you play the game." That is what we are told, but how often is that actually the case? We take a glimpse at our lives and realize that we are much more passionate about getting results than how we play the game. We like results, and when we get them, it confirms to us that we're doing something right. However, when we as sons hear that it's not about the results, but rather how we play the game, we are left asking what the point is. Does God see it this way? Does God desire us to be more passionate about the character we display than the outward results of our effort? That sound like the opposite of what I should be worried about. But it's true. God wants us to be more passionate about the way in which we live our lives than the outward results that may seem appealing to the culture. It's how you play the game that matters.

You see, we ought to be passionate about how we're living our lives instead of the outward results of money, success, fame, or comfort. God is much more concerned with our heart in the midst of our passion. Are we doing this for God or for ourselves? Am I passionate about this just because everyone else is, or is God in the center of it?

It's tough as a young man to keep that in check. We want our passions to lead us to something great, such as money, fame, and success. However, when our passions are constant with God's leading, our passions become more then a tool to make life meaningful they become a gift that we can use to fulfill our ultimate purpose of imaging

God and reflecting His character. "It's not whether you win or lose, it's how you play the game."

Destructive Passion

However, not all passion is good, even if it's directed at the right things. A passion for evangelism is a gift from God, but when young reckless Christians try to confront people for their sins, we realize that some passion can be misdirected. Passion is like mental energy. God designed us to be able to put this energy towards living for Him, but this energy needs to be channeled and guided. Unguided passion, while well meaning, can be destructive. As a father, I encourage you not to try to snuff out your son's passion, but rather to help guide and direct it into productive use. Think again of the son who has a great passion for evangelism and yet is harshly confrontational in his encounters with unbelievers. What are you, as his father, supposed to do? You don't what to dampen his passion for sharing the gospel by confronting him. You know that he'll mature eventually and grow out of this recklessness, but you also don't want him representing Christ the way he is. This is a conundrum for sure. Give me the pleasure of telling you something that your son would want you to know. He doesn't have this thing figured out, he just wants to be passionate about something that matters. However, he doesn't necessarily know what godly passion looks like. Helping to guide and direct your son's passion is a sensitive task. Your fear keeps you from acting as you don't want to do any unnecessarily harmful in confronting him. Thus, you leave him in the dark hoping his misguided passion will one day be transformed into a healthy, godly, correctly motivated passion. Please, don't leave him in the dark. Are young men stubborn? Many are. But please do not take that as a license to step back. He wants to know what it looks like to be passionate about something that matters. He wants to hear what it sounds like to be passionate about God. He's going to get off track. Give him respect by gently talking to him.

Productive Passion

Young men care and stare. They can care about what matters, but they too often sit, stare, and stay. This often characterizes our lives as sons. We're passionate, but we appreciate the position of benchwarmer, or more accurately, we prefer to sit on our couch watching the game on television. A passion that stays on the couch is useless. You can say something matters to you, you can believe it in your heart, you can study up on all the facets of something that fascinates you, and yet you can still sit. What use is a passion if it doesn't show creation its maker? What good is a passion if it is kept to ourselves?

You want your son to be passionate, but does it matter if he follows through? We talk a big game. We say we need to hold to good theology and yet haven't picked up our Bible this week. We say we're passionate about good stories and yet rarely pick up a pen (or keyboard). We say we're passionate about being in a real Christ-centered community, yet we rarely go out of our way to make it happen. Your son likes comfort as much as you do. The couch is warm, comfortable, and enticing. We like it when our passion allows us to stay there, but meaningful passions need to be followed through in a tangible way. Your son's passionate about good theology? Encourage him to use it. Speak it. Teach it. Meaningful passions must be expressed. However, that kind of action takes real work. This is where we encounter the gap between those who say they're passionate about something and those who actually do something. You want your son to be in the latter group. You want his passions to be productive. However, it isn't always straightforward.

Through my teen years, I loved learning about theology, hearing people talk about living the Christian life, and listening to Christians use media to talk about the cause of Christ. I had a passion for it, but that was where it stopped. For a long time, the extent of my passion was to make sure I was caught up on all the blogs and articles that had been released by the people I was following. Don't get me wrong, this isn't an innately bad thing. It's okay to consume other people's content and admire where their passion has taken them so you can learn from it, but real passion ought to lead us towards something greater.

I was overwhelmed. How could I use the passion I had for communicating with people about Jesus and the Christian walk? I was young, had a lot of questions, and felt inadequate. Your son may be in the same position. For me it took a friend prompting me toward a practical step to getting my content out there. Be this friend for your son; he may be overwhelmed. Guide him to turn his passive passion to a productive one.

Purposeful, Inspired Passion

I've been talking about living for something greater and being inspired to live for Christ. I've also talked about living with purpose. Our ultimate purpose to glorify God and image Him on this earth. In this chapter, I've talked quite a bit about passion and how we ought to use it to further God's kingdom. All those concepts go hand in hand. We need to be inspired to live for something greater so that we can find our purpose and live it out passionately.

These three concepts are so central to living the Christian walk and yet many fathers never speak of such things to their sons. Sons are given instructions, but they want to know why. Why is that important? Sons are told to do something, but they need to know how. How do I focus my energy on my passions? Do you have the answers? Your son is finding it difficult to piece this together on his own. Explaining how passion and purpose intermingle can not only help him as he tries to make sense of what he's doing and why he's doing it, but it can help your son see you as a vital encourager in this process.

See the passion in your son as a tool that needs to be directed and guided. Many young men put their passions toward things that are not of God. Pornography, jealousy, anger, and fame are just some of the many passions that may tempt your son. "So flee youthful passions and pursue righteousness, faith, love, and peace, along with those who call on the Lord from a pure heart." 2 Timothy 2:22. Encourage your son in this, that he may use his passion for God's glory and live it out with purpose!

LETTER 7:
Difference Maker

Dear Dad,

As I write this to you, I feel stuck, like I'm trapped in a reality where I am unable to do anything important. I want to make a difference, but I feel like it's not going to happen. I'm doing things that I don't feel matter or that don't seem to make a difference. I'm confused. Why wouldn't God help me do something big for Him, something spectacular, to make a difference for Him? But yet I'm here doing things that seem insignificant and make me feel like just giving up. Even when opportunities arise, I question whether God would actually be able to use me. What if I fail? What if I don't have what it takes to make a defense? What if I get stuck doing insignificant things my whole life? What if I never make a difference for God? Sometimes

> the weight of those questions leads me to try
> not to care. I need you to try to understand.
> I don't really get why life is this way. We can
> have great desires to change the world and yet
> we're left wanting. I'm looking for answers.
>
> Love,
> Your Son

The world moves. Its first movement, at the hands of God, pushed it into motion. Still, we humans try to move it in a different direction. Sin has corrupted our world and thus a spiritual tug of war has begun. God has already won. Still, we pull.

I want to make a difference on this earth for good—for God. Young men fantasize of saving their family from home intruders, stopping a gunman from hurting helpless civilians, and arriving in the nick of time to do away with the bad guys. We are heroes—if only in our minds.

However, other fantasies make their home in our hopeful minds: Impacting someone's life towards Christ. Giving people hope through the message of the gospel. Acting, inventing, saying something to change the world and make a difference. We stand hopeful—some would say ignorantly so, but you know better. I hope you do.

Your son wants to make a difference. This is something to be excited about as a father, but also realize that the road ahead isn't going to be easy. It's wonderful to have good desires like making a difference, but sometimes our expectations of what that looks like get in the way of us seeing what God's doing through us. Let me continue this chapter with a story.

Something Big

The lineup for the McDonald's drive-through was annoyingly long. It was nine o'clock at night. It was either a milkshake plus a twenty-minute wait, or head home and hope there's something good to eat there. I chose the latter. It seemed like a responsible decision. I had just got off my shift at a local grocery store and I was not about to put off getting some rest. I made my way home for what was about a five-minute drive. It was a late shift, so I was happy to get to use my parents' vehicle that night, also because it was pouring rain. Rain sets a mood. It really does. As rain hits the windshield, you began to feel like you're in a movie—the beginning of a movie before anything really has happened. The exciting part comes later, or so I'd hoped.

I parked my parents' vehicle on our front street and got out of the car, but made no attempt to get out of the rain quickly. It was almost a sign of surrender, like I had given up. I was miserable, working in large freezers and fridges with what seemed like a never-ending load of work every shift. It felt like this job was draining the life out of me. I had been at my grocery store job for a few months at this point, but it had felt like years.

There was nothing good in the fridge—great. Perhaps if I kept looking, something of merit will materialize based on my wishes, but I had yet to see that work. To be honest, I was demoralized, not because there was nothing good in the fridge, though that was cause for disappointment. My job was the real problem. I hated it.

There was nothing good on TV. I changed the channel too fast to register what was actually playing, but I had had it.

Looking back on it now, there was no reason based on the job itself that led to my dislike of it, but it would come into focus soon.

As I sat hoping to find something worthwhile on TV, I heard the familiar sound of the stairs creaking. I had assumed everyone had gone to sleep. My dad crept down the stairs and wandered into the kitchen. He turned on the kettle (which only happened when he was making Mom tea), and then peered into the fridge as I had moments before.

"How was work?" he asked as his head reappeared from behind the fridge door.

"Not good. It was boring and stressful at the same time." My fingers touched the top of my forehead. "I just couldn't wait for it to be done." Dad turned to get a mug out of the cupboard as he silently anticipated that I was not done my piece. "I just don't understand it. I want to do something meaningful, something that impacts people." I took a breath. "No one's life has been changed because of how I packed the food on the grocery store shelves." Dad gave me a look that brought me back to when I was a kid. The only way I can explain it is when you're a kid, your parents expect a certain amount of ignorance and idealism. Their attitude is not necessary condescending, but their smile says, "You have a lot to learn, kid." That's the kind of look he gave me. I wanted to make a difference, and I didn't think working at a grocery store would be my road to do that.

There are times in your life that you tone down what you think and how you feel to avoid coming across as extreme, but this was not one of those times. I said what I felt.

"You know, Isaac, not every job will be meaningful and fulfilling, especially when you're young."

What? I want to do something big for God, something meaningful, and I'm supposed to believe that this job is where God wants me right now. I couldn't believe it.

"Later on, you'll find a job where you can have the impact you want, but it'll be a journey to get there."

A journey? I wanted to make an impact now! I wanted to change the world now! Regardless, I went to bed that night still confused.

Many sons are frustrated. We want to make a difference. We want to do something big for God. Do we know what that looks like? Maybe not. But still, we have that longing. We sometimes feel stuck doing things that seem useless in the grand scheme of things. Do we just hope that someday we will make a difference? That someday, we'll do something meaningful? Someday, we'll do something big for God?

Something Small

Your son wants to make a difference. He may not know how or why, but he does, and if he's anything like I was, he wants to do it now! Many sons have a "now mentality."

We like things to be quick, easy, and convenient. We don't like to wait, and we don't like to hear about the struggle associated with getting to where we want to be. Not only do we want our impact to be felt now, we want it to be massive and life changing. But we're not there yet. We're working jobs that we don't find meaningful and living lives that are falling short of spectacular. It doesn't feel fair to many young men. But there is missing information. God doesn't want "big" from us, he wants faithful. He doesn't want sons to arrive without a journey, He wants us to trust Him.

Our ideas of doing something big for God are nothing compared to the plans that God has for us. That doesn't mean they're big plans, but they are meaningful. That is, in faithfully working and serving where we are, we can find purpose in making a meaningful difference for the kingdom of God. So even in the midst of my grocery store job, I could be faithful to God and make a meaningful difference in people's lives by showing them a glimpse of the character of God through His work in my life. Making a difference for God isn't necessarily outwardly heroic, spectacular, or life changing, but it is faithful. God has called both you and your son to faithfulness.

This line of thinking does not only relate to your job but to all other areas of your life as well. You can think of the people that had the most impact on you when you were younger, and you are mostly brought back to people that faithfully contributed to your life. This impact likely wasn't brought about by a one-time thing that they did or said, but rather a consistent, faithful involvement in your life. This is both instructive for you as a father, as you try to affect your son's life, and for your son, as he tries to affect other people's lives. I want to emphasize this legacy of faithfulness that you want to pass down to your son. Real lasting impact is laid down after years of faithfulness regardless of how "big" the thing you are doing is. Your son still might not understand that yet, it's taken me until recently to really begin to understand that. Take time to show him that making a difference begins in the small, faithful stuff.

He Doesn't Care

You feel stuck. I told you that your son wants to make a difference, but I also realize that you may have a different experience with your own son. Perhaps he has shown a concerning amount of apathy over the last couple of months or years. He doesn't seem to care. Why? You consider the media he's consuming. You know he has a tendency toward the cynical side, and he tends to gravitate to content that reflects that. You think about his friends. They seem like good kids and yet you're positive that one of these things is leading your son into this disheartening apathy. Regardless, it's starting to frustrate you. You read books, listen to podcasts, go to seminars, go on father-son campouts, but it doesn't seem to make a difference. You feel stuck. Why doesn't he seem to care? What I'm I supposed to do?

Take a breath. Let's go back to basics. Sometimes in the midst of our expectations, we lack communicating them. You want your son to want to make a difference for

God, but have you told him why he should care? Seriously, as a father, it's easy to enter the world of unspoken expectations. These usually breed frustration on both sides. Communicate with your son. Tell your son where you're at and what you want for him. Be loving, but clear. Only God can change his heart, but you can help communicate your expectations by telling him what you want for him. You want him to care. Tell him why. This is a simple concept, yet incredibly hard to follow through with. It is uncomfortable to communicate the expectations you have, yet extremely worthwhile with the clarity that will be established. Communicate with him and wait for him in the midst of his apathy. I'll talk more about that in the next chapter. For now, I want to go back to the son who wants to make a difference.

Show Him Where He Can

Your son may know that making a difference isn't necessarily about the heroic, spectacular, big stuff, yet he will still yearn for a place and time to live out his purpose with passion to make a difference.

How do you help him do that?

Many books give great concepts and principles yet neglect to give practical advice. I want to avoid that mistake here.

Where is there a need in your son's sphere of influence? Remember, making a difference is about more than just being a hero, it's about being faithful. Is there a need that you see that your son could play a role in meeting? Perhaps your son has a particular area of work or service that he is most passionate about. Have you looked for opportunities for him? I know this sounds like common sense. However, going out of your way to look for opportunities for him gives him a clear message that you believe in him and want to help him. Showing him an opportunity may be the turning point in your son's quest to make a difference. He wants to make a difference, show him how he can.

When you suggest an opportunity to your son, you help to give him the confidence to go for it. If all else fails, he knows at least one person believes in him and the difference he can make. That goes a long way.

Your son might think, what if I'm not equipped? What if I fail? What if I can't make a difference? These and other questions race through our minds as opportunities arise. Young men have looming questions over their heads. What if I'm not enough? What if I can't?

A I write this, I am sitting on the deck of my parents' house. A red beach umbrella next to me provides enough shade to make out the words on the screen. A ray of sunlight breaks through and exposes the building dust on my keyboard. The process of writing this book has been filled with questions. Rightfully so. Worthwhile things are often those that we question the most. We question their meaning. We question our motives. We question ourselves. I have questions. What if I can't? What if I can't help fathers affect their sons' lives? What if I can't make this book compelling enough to read? What if no one buys this book, rendering the time spent writing it a waste? What if this book doesn't affect fathers and sons toward a more Christ-like relationship? I feel the weight of my desires weighing on me. I try to restrain my hopes for the possibility of being disappointed. Failure is peering at me.

We tend to brace for failure so we don't get disappointed. We want to make a difference, but what if we can't? We are then confronted with the truth. Questions of self-doubt surround us and yet God is calling us to be his tools. We still have questions, but we surrender to God in trust, believing He can work through us. God can use us to make a difference. He will, but it may not look like what we thought it would. This is so hard to come to terms with. If God is all powerful, wouldn't he help us to do something big for Him? Something impactful? Yet I'm led to believe that even in the midst of what looks like failure, God is at work. He is the difference maker; we are His tools. Our perspective is limited. We want to do something now, something big, something impactful, but sometimes we can't see what's really going on. God is at work in our midst.

Your son's perspective is limited, you know that, so it might be harder for his young eyes to see what God is doing. He may be discouraged and demoralized. He may have given up. Sometimes caring comes with a weight too heavy to bear on our own. Are you on his team? He wants to be the hero, world changer, difference maker, yet he feels that his desires are left unmet. Come with understanding in supply and a keen eye on God's perspective. Help him see it. God is at work in the world, in his life, and in your life. Don't give up. Continue on this journey with your son. You're making a difference in his life. God is at work.

LETTER 8:
Wait for Me

Dear Dad,

Can I be honest with you? I know I'm not the perfect son. I know I disappoint you. I know I let you down. I'm sorry. But sometimes I just feel angry. Sometimes I feel like I don't belong. Sometimes I feel like you judge my every decision. I get to the point of giving up or wanting to run away. I think you mean well, but it feels like I get a lot more of sighs than excitement from you. It makes me feel like I'm not wanted, like all I'm good for is what I can do or accomplish. I'm still trying to figure all this out and running sometimes seems like the right move. I know that makes you angry. You blame yourself, you're frustrated, but so am I. I guess I'm asking you to wait for me. I know I don't deserve it, but I don't know, could you just hold on for bit?

> I'm trying to figure this out. Could you wait for me?
>
> Love,
> Your Son

At one point in our lives, we were runners. We suppressed the truth as we ran from our Maker. Pride, self-sufficiency, and love for sin drove us further from God as we ran away at our own peril. Selfishly, we used our God-given talents and gifts for our own personal gain, as we recklessly abandoned God's call for our life. Yet, when God transformed our hearts, we were able to see our sin in light of God's perfect character, which led us to repentance and faith in Him. For many of us, this was a slow and gradual process in which God was drawing us to Himself. His patient love was drawing us home. He waited for us. Though we didn't deserve it, He waited for us.

In Luke 15, Jesus tells of the parable of the prodigal son, in which the younger of the two sons asked his father for his share of the inheritance. His father gave him the inheritance and the son then journeyed far away and proceeded to squander his money in irresponsible and sinful living. After his money ran out, he was forced to eat with the pigs to survive. He was broke. He had wasted his father's hard-earned money, which was given to him as a gift. Anyone looking in from the outside would agree that this son certainly did not deserve any kind of grace. He was the epitome of a rebellious son.

As the story continues, the son then decided to return to his father and to ask him to hire him like a lowly slave.

That is all he could ask for after what he had done. When he returned home and after reciting his pre-rehearsed speech of repentance and request to be a lowly slave, his father met him with a response that he was not expecting. His father met him with love, joy, and excitement. His father called for a great feast and organized a celebration for the son. No one could have predicted such a response. Looking in, we might have expected a response of judgment and shaming: "How could you waste all the money that I gave you?" Or perhaps a response of anger and rage: "I can't believe what you've done, how could you do this?" Or a response of rejection: "You are not welcome here. You have wasted all I have given you. I want nothing to do with you after what you have done." Instead, Jesus flips the narrative to help us understand His character. Not only that, He teaches us how we ought to respond to the rebels in our own life. The father had waited for the son in expectation of his arrival home, and was prepared to rejoice with him because of it. God is telling us to wait in anticipation for the rebel because He waited for us.

Most Christians are readily familiar with the parable of the prodigal son. We understand that God is the father and we are the reckless son. God waited for us when we didn't deserve it, when we wasted what he gave us, when we turned to sin and ran from home. We're eternally grateful that He did. However, as a father, you still wonder how you can begin to model the kind of love that the father did in the parable. In this chapter, we're going to dig into how you can do that.

Runners

As a father, you try to do the best you can. You try to create a gospel-centered atmosphere within your home, foster godly behavior, teach the truth, answer questions, forgive mistakes, correct, love, and more. You hope that it'll all be enough to help lead your son on his way to a life filled with a passion for God and a love for His ways. You would like to think that if you teach him the truth, he will listen. If you explain godly living, he will understand and live it out. If you pray for him, he'll turn out exactly as you wanted and expected. You have the expectation of God that if you do your part—try to raise him well—God will do His and bless you with the son you dreamed of. It makes sense to us: do your part, God will do His. But it didn't turn out as you expected. As much as you try to be the perfect godly father, your son won't be the perfect godly son. In fact, he may run. He'll run from you, from God, or from home with his inheritance.

You thought you did well. You read all the books, went to all the parenting conferences, went on the father-son retreats, made sure he had good friendship influences, talked with him, and yet he is running away from you and God. If this is you, take a breath, I want to talk to you. If this is not you, I still believe that you'll benefit from our conversation in this chapter.

Why We Run

Why is this happening? You question whether it was something you said or something you did that led him to this kind of rebellion. You get angry with him. You get angry with yourself. You remember times of failure when you weren't patient with him. Times that you weren't understanding of what he was going through. Times where guidance given was more like a harsh rant than godly correction. You ask yourself what you did wrong.

Why do some sons rebel? Sin, selfishness, anger, greed? Yes. Being hurt, receiving harsh judgment, feeling neglected, being scared? Yes. Those are all reasons that sons rebel. What can you as a father do? You tried your best, yet your son is still going astray. Which one is the cause of his actions, behavior, and belief? I don't know. I wish I could tell you the exact cause, it would make things infinitely easier (and me significantly richer), but I can't. What I can do is highlight some of the big issues that relate to rebellion and how you can care for your son even in the midst of it.

I want to make clear that sin is always ways a factor, for both parties. Sons blame fathers and claim to have been wronged. Fathers accuse sons of selfishness and pride, leading them to rebellion. Sons feel like they're not wanted or not important, so they rebel to find belonging elsewhere. Fathers blame themselves and allow anger to mask the pain. Who is at fault? You? Your son? Your sin? His sin? Yes, yes, yes, and yes. Sin is at play. Our hearts are quick to accuse, quick to anger, quick to bitterness, and quick to blame. Understand that this isn't an exercise of calling you out as a bad father. Neither is this an opportunity to give you license to wipe your hands clean of your son's rebellion. I want you to understand your son. Do you want that? Do you want to meet him where he is? I hope so, because he needs you. Let's keep moving.

Hypocrisy

An excuse for sin. That is often what we're dealing with. More often than not, your failure as a father does not directly lead to your son's rebellion, but rather, gives him an excuse for why he can rebel. This is the case for the issue of hypocrisy. I told you earlier that your son has a gift in sensing hypocrisy. He may very well use your failures as justification for his actions. "If Dad can't even live this Christian life, why should I try? If Dad can't walk the talk, why should I?" Your son may be thinking that your sin is an excuse for his. If he sees you talking big about your spiritual merit and yet he sees your failure, he may grow angry. How do you avoid this? You could be perfect, but we know that's not an option. My encouragement to you is the same as in the second chapter: be real. When you're real with him, it disarms his excuses. You are going to make mistakes. You are going to sin. But when you are real with your son about the way you try to live your life and the forgiveness found in Christ, you take away his excuses. Your son may still rebel, but it is important that you are real with your son about your failings as you try to guide him towards Christ.

Judgment

Do you care about your son? You say, "Of course, I'm reading this book after all." Does your son know that you care? You think, "Sure he knows. I don't need to spell it out for him, he gets it." Has your interaction with him, which you understood as tough love, become a life of tough love with him? Maybe you come across as more angry than caring. Maybe the love that you think you are showing through your comments to him comes off as more cutting than loving. Does he feel more judged than loved? We are called to speak the truth in love, and yet we often don't really have a concept of what that practically looks like.

Perhaps your son is already in the midst of rebellion. Ideas and tactics rush to your mind—a few helpful, most you disregard—and you look for an answer in how to respond. Do you come across as stern to make sure he knows you're serious? Do you preach the gospel to him in hopes that he'll turn from his ways? Do you pray that he'll come to his senses and in the meanwhile try to act like everything's okay, even in the midst of his rebellion? Do you try to love him unconditionally, even in the midst of the pain he's causing you and your family as a whole? You push too hard and he'll run farther; not enough and he'll never change. You feel stuck.

First, I would encourage you to look at your ruling emotion in the interactions with your son regarding his rebellion. Do you have a ruling emotion of anger and judgment towards his behavior? Or maybe you have mixed emotions of disappointment and discouragement? Or do you have a ruling emotion of love towards him that leads you to have concern for his soul and his life in general? This is important to understand. The emotions that you approach him with are what he'll get out of it. If you approach him in anger, he will feel anger. If you approach him with judgment, he'll feel judged. If you approach him in love, there is a good chance he will feel loved. You want him to change, but what will lead him there? Is it anger? Judgment? Your anger and judgment will just lead him to shame. Will shame lead him home? No, shame draws him away. Shame tells him he is not wanted. Shame tells him he could never be forgiven. Shame tells him he does not belong. Shame tells him to hide from you and from God. Anger and judgment tell him to run. Understanding and love tell him to stay a while. Let's talk, let's figure this out. Understanding and love tell him he's wanted.

We think back to the prodigal son and look at the father's response to his return. The father wasn't fostering the shame already present in the son's life. Instead, he welcomed him home with love and understanding. Yes, the son repented, but it may be a while before your son comes around. Wait for him even in the midst of his rebellion. Show him that same love that the father showed the son in that story and that same love that God had for us while we ran from him.

Welcome

Where do you go to find your sense of belonging? People might say their friends, their job, or their family. There is something profound in God's design of the family. Similar to the church, each member of a family has a role to play and a place in which they can belong. This hunger for belonging can be so strong that many dedicate their lives to fulfilling this desire. We avoid places where we feel we don't have that sense of belonging. We avoid groups of people if we feel we don't belong. We gravitate to those who take us in, who make us feel like we belong, that we have value in being there.

Your son wants to belong, just like you do. During the adolescent and young adult stage, this quest to belong is at the forefront of their minds. They not only want to fit in, but they want to be wanted, they want to be valued. The family is designed so that each member is valued and wanted, but too often today, even within Christian families and churches, sons are left feeling out of place. Not wanted. Not valued. They feel like they don't belong. Shame tells him he doesn't belong. He listens. Rebellion is sometimes only a consequence in the quest for belonging. Keep in mind that there is no justification for sinful rebellion, but it is our reality. It's a God-given desire to want to belong. We were made to operate in a body of many people with different strengths and roles. Each feeling is valued and loved, but shame has distorted our desire. Young men may rebel against what they know in their hearts is right with the hope that they will find that sense of belonging somewhere else. Understand this in your son and begin to show him that he is not only welcome, but he belongs.

Hope He'll Come Around

A man stands on his porch and the front door is partially cracked. It's dark and the porch light is the only light in sight. He stands in the light. The cool night's breeze would send shivers down anyone's spin, but this man is not fazed. His attention is elsewhere. He had been standing there for what seemed like an eternity. His body, warmed by his coat; his feet, socks with slippers. He had woken up in the middle of the night, tiptoed downstairs to the front porch with hopes of not waking up his wife, but that was not at the forefront of his mind. Looking at him, you could see something was wrong. It may have been the bags under his eyes, which looked as if they had been there for many nights. The face of worry is not easily hidden and his was certainly not. His son, where is his son? He had left the night before, an argument left them at odds. One trying to guide and correct, one feeling attacked and rejected, two left angry and worried. The father waits and hopes. Will he come home? Will God bring my son back? The sound of the front door opening breaks the man out of his thoughts. His wife comes out through the door. She understands. No words are needed. She comes to his side and he sighs. They wait and hope that he would come around. There's nothing left to say. Nothing left to do. They just pray for their son to come home. Unconditional love. Patient love. Yes, this was God's prescription. A painful love.

Waiting for your son will not be easy. In fact, it may be the hardest thing you've ever had to do. God will give you strength. Remember that those who rebel will rarely return when all they hear is a voice of judgment. Keep your doors open and wait for him. This kind of love is painful. It makes your heart groan for God to intervene. It will take patience and self-control. Your son won't ask you to wait for him. In fact, he may tell you not to. I'll ask for him: wait for him, because through you, he is beginning to get a glimpse of God, the father, welcoming him home with forgiveness, understanding, and love. That's all he could ask for.

LETTER 9:
Girls, Purity, and Waiting

Dear Dad,

In writing these letters, I've kept coming back to this topic in my mind, but I kept avoiding writing this letter because it felt too awkward. I guess I finally feel like it's time to stop putting it off. I know we don't talk about this stuff very much, but I'm having a hard time. I feel like I'm constantly confronted with the temptation to fall into sexual sin—pornography, stuff in movies and TV, going too far with girls—and my heart seems to be drawn to everything that God is against. The battle is real, and I feel like I lose a lot more than I win. I know God has designed these desires for marriage, and yet I find waiting to be agonizing at times. Being content right now seems to be imposable. Like I said before, I know we don't really talk about this stuff, but I'm running out of people to turn to. My friends seem to feel the same pull towards sexual sin, but we never would talk about this stuff. I'm looking for some help, to be honest, and I was hoping you might have something to say. Let me know. I'll write again soon.

Love,
Your son

The Talk. We hate talking about this stuff. It's awkward—for both fathers and sons. At least it's "The Talk" and not "The Talks." Fathers have the mentality to say what needs to be said about this subject once and hope to never bring it up again. It's awkward. It's weird. Both fathers and sons would prefer if these issues of purity, girls, relationships, and sexuality were left alone. As the father, you think he'll figure it out. The son thinks, "I'll figure it out." So, fathers and sons stop talking about it. It's not just about having The Talk. It's about whether or not we're going to have an ongoing conversation about these things. Sex, girls, dating, and courting are all things that you may hate talking to your son about, but the question is, does he need to hear from you about them?

When you think about the growing epidemic of pornography addiction, kids dating in their early teens, and young men looking to find a potential spouse, yet have no idea of how to go about doing that in a God-glorifying way, we have to ask ourselves, do fathers have anything to add to their son's journey in this area? Of course they do! For too long, sons have been missing out. Too often, fathers feel uncomfortable when these issues are brought up and they decide to pull away. Because of this, confusion for the son is imminent and guidance on these issues from the father is limited. I don't want that for you or your son.

Throughout this book, we've talked about developing real and authentic communication between fathers and sons. In doing that, we can't pull away when conversations are becoming uncomfortable. As you probably know, often times the most uncomfortable conversations are some of the most important. We need to talk about this stuff. If he doesn't hear it from you, he's hearing it from everyone else. He's hearing that sex is meaningless. He's hearing that purity is lame. He's hearing that men were made to be with many partners over a lifetime. Do you want your voice to be the only one not there? A common theme in this book has been the fact that your son is still trying to figure things out—his purpose, his passion, his goals—and at the same time trying to understand his struggles. Likewise, in the teenage years, the confusion around relationships, dating, courting, and girls is real. So many questions race through his mind. When should I get married? When should I start dating/courting? What kind of girl should I be looking for? How do I stay pure? How do I avoid sexual temptation? What kinds of boundaries are important in a relationship? How do I get into a relationship? So many questions. He may ask you some, yet because of the state of many father-son relationships, it's doubtful he will. By having an ongoing conversation with your son about these things, you'll help open the door for these questions to be asked. Without an ongoing conversation, many questions won't be asked. It's just the way most sons are.

We avoid asking questions that make us feel uncomfortable. However, if you think about the importance of this area of life and essential things that God has to say about it, fathers ought to be eager to engage in conversations with their son about these things that matter to God. It may be uncomfortable, but let's began to tear down those walls of awkwardness so that we can help each other on our journey together. That's where we need to begin. Not just with "a talk," but with an ongoing conversation. It's important to God, so it ought to be important to us.

Eleven Years Old

When I was eleven years old, I had a friend who I'm going to call Liam. I knew Liam from the triathlon team that I mentioned earlier. He was about my age and faster than I was in biking and running, but not swimming. It was my one claim to fame that I was always first after the swimming portion of the race. Was I passed by almost every person participating throughout the rest of the race? Yes, but I don't like to dwell on that.

It was Saturday and the bike training session was about to start. This entailed biking a loop around a large park. To pass the time we would often break into groups of two to talk as we biked. I paired up with Liam and we were on our way. Little did I know that during our forty-minute bike ride, I was about to hear about his experience in sex ed. I don't really remember any of the specifics of what he said; all of it went right over my head. I was just confused. Like, REALLY confused. I don't think this kind of experience was an anomaly. There's a good possibility that your son is going to hear about this stuff from one of his friends or someone else.

This is why I say to start the conversation early. Use wisdom, but don't let discomfort or awkwardness get in the way of you talking to your son about these important topics. Hearing this stuff from their father sends them the message that you are trying to walk with your son through what he is going through and trying to help. When these issues of purity, dating, marriage, and relationships are avoided in the home, a disconnection begins to develop in the mind of the son. "Why do my friends talk about this stuff, but my parents don't? Are these topics shameful in some way? Does my dad even know what I'm going through?" Don't ignore the relevance of these topics, even if your son isn't at the marrying or dating age. If he feels like you are ignoring these issues, he's either going to feel alone and figure it out on his own or look to other people for their thoughts. Most of the time, these thoughts come from their friends, and as you can see, friends at that age aren't the best for this kind of wisdom. You are. God has designed you to be the one for him to go to. Be intentional about having those conversations with him.

Thirteen Years Old

I'm going to preface this story by saying that I am not a "normal" person. Part of the challenge of writing this book is discerning what is common among most sons and what is just my weirdness. I'll explain.

When I was thirteen years old, I got into listening to different pastors and teachers on YouTube. I would listen all the time. A few preachers I could not get enough of, including Pastor Voddie Baucham. I was looking for answers. I was hitting puberty and wanted to know what all this relationship stuff was all about. I typed into YouTube something like "when do you get married? Voddie Baucham." In seconds, I was watching a sermon about preparing for marriage. Keep in mind, I was thirteen. The sermon talked about the different things that are important to get in place before you get married. Things like your relationship with God, your family relationships, your finances. One of these things was that if you want to get married, you need a job. My first thought as a thirteen-year-old was, "Well, I guess I need to a job." I'm weird, I know, but that isn't to say that other young men don't have that desire to be in a relationship, even in their teen years. We like girls—it's the way God made us—but we aren't sure how to be in a relationship or when the right time is. I wanted to be married when I was thirteen—not really, I knew it wasn't going to be soon, but that desire was still there. I want you, as a father, to understand that you may assume that your son's not thinking about this stuff, but he is. Whether he has a desire to get married at thirteen is another question, but he is thinking about these topics.

A Letter to My Father

Purity

As you begin this ongoing conversation, you want your son to be honoring God in these areas of his life. Hopefully he wants that as well. This is where we start, with an ongoing conversation about this area of life with a focus on honor God at the center. How do we honor God in relationships, dating, courting, and being single? I believe the main area that we can do that is with our sexual purity. Too often, fathers see this as a topic that can be addressed when their son is seventeen or eighteen, when really the conversation needs to begin much earlier. You might think of sexual purity as merely a physical thing, but Jesus certainly didn't.

"You have heard that it was said, 'You shall not commit adultery.' But I say to you that everyone who looks at a woman with lustful intent has already committed adultery with her in his heart." Matthew 5:27-28 ESV

Jesus sees what happens in our heart as just as important about what we do with our physical bodies. We ought to have that same emphasis on what goes on in our hearts, even from an early age. This is why I think it is so important that you began thing conversation early.

There are so many important truths that you can share with your son about issues of sexuality and relationships, but I also want to stress that as you help your son pursue purity, you also want to focus on helping him develop some practical habits of purity in his life.

For you as a married man, what are the things that you won't do, places where you won't go, things that you won't watch, conversations that you won't engage in? What are some of your habits of pursuing purity in your own life? What are the practical things that you do or don't do in an effort to stay away from temptation and pursue Christ? Think about it. As we get older, the habits that we hold begin to form our lives more and more. The good ones lead us to Christ, the bad ones may be new, or perhaps have been hanging on as we try to smother the life out of them. Habits form our lives, including that of your son. Now think again. What are some of the habits that you try to maintain about sexual purity, physically, and at the heart level? Do you think you could help pass this habit on to your son? Even in his early teens, he is beginning to form habits about how he responds to temptation and what he watches, listens to, and engages in. These habits are going to be his foundation and how he pursues purity in his life. My encouragement to you is that you would instill in your son the habits that you have developed in pursuing purity. Yes, he could figure these things out on his own, but think back to your struggles concerning this issue if you had them. If you want your son to be more equipped to run from temptation than you were, be there for him so he can be.

As much as I want you to help your son through your experiences, as you remember how you now deal with it and how you did when you were younger, when you dealt with sexual temptation, I want you to understand that the world your son is living in is much different from what it was. Perhaps you may be younger, and this change has not been so drastic. Regardless, the world your son is living in now is one that has sexual temptation down every corner. Turn on a computer and you have the means to look at things that will destroy your soul. Many movies portray women as objects to be used rather than people to be loved and understood. We live in a culture that applauds young men for having meaningless sex with as many women as they can. We are in an uphill battle. For your son, this may be the fight of his life. Join him in this battle early, before it's too late.

Not Yet

An hourglass sits, its particles of sand fall, reminding us that time is moving. The sand in the hourglass piles up, telling us of the time we've already spent. The sand still at the top is the time we have left, but we can't see how much is there, and it worries us. We sometimes see our lives as a series of big moments that define each chapter. For young men, the wait before being in a romantic relationship with a girl is tough.

The culture around us acts on their feelings. They act on their desires for the relationship, no matter what stage they may be at, or if it's the right person or not. The world says "now" about expressing sexuality and pursuing romantic relationships, but God often says "not yet." This idea can be agonizing for young men.

Sometimes when I talk about waiting, I mean waiting for our sexual desires to be righteously fulfilled in a marriage partner. Other times I'm talking about the general desire to be married and all that comes with it, including sex.

Let's start with the first one. Sometimes within our Christian circles, we treat sexuality as something dirty from which Christians need to clean themselves. The truth is that God created us as sexual beings; however, because of sin, our sexuality has been perverted—that is, we misuse it. Sexuality is not evil, but it can be misdirected.

My dad was good at referring to sexuality in its proper context in our conversations. The idea was that sexuality was not evil, but the phrase "not yet" was common in our conversations. Too many well-meaning fathers, in an attempt to keep their sons on the path of purity, give their sons the impression that sex is a bad thing, like it is something to be shunned. By using clear and truthful language like "not yet" about waiting for marriage, you give your son the tools to understand his sexuality in light of biblical truth. It's so important to make the distinction that sexuality is not evil. Rather, it was designed to be expressed within the loving relationship of marriage. This truth will help clear up a lot of questions your son has about these issues.

As I mentioned earlier, waiting does not only relate to sex but also the general desire to be married as well. At thirteen, I was already dreading waiting until eighteen to get married (God had different plans for me anyway). The idea of marriage can seem extremely enticing. When loneliness can seem to characterize many young men's lives, the idea of living with a girl that you love seems too good to be true. But the wait worries us. We worry that it'll never happen, that if we wait any longer, we'll never get married. As sons, we become impatient. A sixteen-year-old guy sees other guys his age dating and being in romantic relationships with girls and he feels like he is behind in some way. Even older guys that are not in a relationship feel this pressure. There is a tug of war within us; we want to be married, yet we may be too young, or maybe just not ready. We hear family member's questions— "Do you have a girlfriend?"—and the pressure is increased.

What can you as a father do to help your son in all of this? First, it important to realize that as your son is waiting, it's tough for him. However, I want to encourage you to help point your son towards God's purpose in his singleness, whether a teen who wants to date or a young man who wants to get married soon and start a family, God has a purpose for him in his singleness. However, he still may feel pressure to be in a relationship, brought about either by himself or others. I want to encourage you not to be the one to put that pressure on him, but rather to help encourage him while he waits.

A temptation of young men is to focus on getting in a relationship. Some guys jump from one relationship to the next just for fun. Even if that doesn't sound like your son, there may be a temptation for him to let the wait for a romantic relationship distract him. For some guys, the desire to get in a relationship keeps them from being as productive as they could be. As a father, help ease the pressure of him being in a relationship and encourage him not to let the relationship that he doesn't have to distract him from serving God effectively.

I want to note that some guys are happier not being in a relationship. Because not all sons can be put in one box with the same desires all appearing at one stage of their life, it's imperative that you communicate with your son about what he thinks about marriage and relationships. Get status updates about where he's at.

I remember one supper, my dad asked us three oldest boys (my older brother was nineteen, I was sixteen, my younger brother was thirteen), on a scale to one to ten, what is your interest level in girls right now? This was unexpected, as he didn't often ask things like that in those years. My answer was three, but it was actually more like an eight. Nevertheless, he was interested in hearing about where we were at.

It's good to talk about biblical truth about purity and what God says about marriage, but take the time and help apply those truths to where your son is now. Perhaps he's a teen seeing his friend beginning to date. He knows that he wants to wait until he's older, but that longing is still there. By getting these status updates, you can help encourage your son, especially concerning what he's feeling and experiencing. That's when the impact of a father is most utilized in your son's life.

Your son is trying to figure this stuff out. It complicated, it's messy, it's confusing, but you can be his window into clarity. You won't have all the answers, but that's not what he's looking for. He's looking for a father who can meet him where he's at and bring him wisdom through God's power. Waiting is hard, purity is hard, relationships are hard, but your son needs to hear that it's worth it. Do you believe it is? Do you believe pursuing God's ways in these areas is worthwhile? Your son may be in the battle of his life, and he needs you in his corner. Are you willing to be? Are you ready to be? You think you're not enough. You think you're not equipped. Perhaps you came to Christ later in life and you're not sure how this is supposed to look biblically. You have doubt that you can help your son. These doubts and question pull you away from your calling in your son's life. Don't give up, push back. God has equipped you and will continue to do so to help and guide your son in this area. God will supply. This is easy to say, but hard to believe. I want to encourage you that in every step you take with your son, every conversation, every interaction, God will continue to grow you and grant you the wisdom to make an impact in your son's life. I truly believe that. Do you? Hope so, because he needs you.

LETTER 10:
Friend or Father?

Dear Dad,

You know since I began writing you these letters, there has been one question that I just can't shake: are you my friend or are you just my father? I'm not sure. We don't talk as much as we used to and when we do, we don't really talk—like really talk. It feels like there's a wall between us somehow. I feel like our relationship is limited to you giving me your evaluation of my choices and decisions. Sometimes it feels like you only talk at me, but never with me. We haven't had a good conversation in a while. I feel like it's my fault because for so long I acted like I wanted nothing to do with you. But now I feel like I really need you. I guess I'm asking for a friend and a father. I don't know if that's too much to ask, but I thought I'd give it a shot. Let me know.

Love,
Your Son

Friends. Good ones are hard to come by. Bad ones seem to be in unlimited supply. We look to our friends for advice, company, laughter, connection, and more. We need friends. Men, however, seem to have a much harder time maintaining close friends as they get older. Friendships are hard. However, good friends are worth the work.

When we think about any relationship or friendship, there needs to be a balance between light and heavy conversation. This is important. If interactions always go deep when talking to a friend, that friendship will become draining. However, if the interactions are always light, the friendship will become trite and feel superficial. There is a balance.

Relationships are a balancing act. I hope I haven't given you the idea that the father-son relationship is only about having tough conversations or only about talking about the heavy issues. In this chapter, I want to set the record straight.

Friend or Father?

"You're his father, not his friend." Has someone told you this before about your son? Maybe you heard a well-meaning speaker say this in an attempt to help you enact some tough love on your son. This is a common line of thinking in fatherhood: don't just act like a friend to your

A Letter to My Father

son, but act like a father. Usually, what those who say these are implying is that you can't just be a friend to your son, but you need to be a father, in that you have tough conversations, you correct him when he's gone astray, and you guide him into wisdom. I do realize there's an important difference in the role of a friend and a father. A friend might not necessarily have the guts to call you out on something, while a father hopefully will. As a father, it's important to have hard conversations; to correct, to call out. However, I think there needs to be an understanding of balance in the father-son relationship.

Some fathers see their role as strictly the authority of their son. They guide, correct, and call them out, but that seems to be the extent of the relationship. Sometimes fathers can get in the ditch of only talking *to* their sons, instead of talking with them. When all that is heard from the father by the son is "do this," "don't do that," "try harder," or "good work," the relationship becomes like an employee and boss. The son feels as though his main goal is to meet the expectations of his father and conform as quickly to do so. The other alternative is that he losses heart after missing the mark to many times and resorts towards rebellion. This is merely a kind of command-response relationship. I hope you can begin to see why this type of father-son relationship can be so damaging. It is stifled when it only consists of doing or not doing. Your son doesn't just need you to be a moral compass; he needs you to be a real friend.

Some people get nervous when you start talking about fathers being their son's friend because they perceive some kind of compromise happening about correction or discipline in the relationship. However, the idea of a father being a friend to his son should not worry us. A true friend has tough conversations. A true friend will call you out when you're wrong. A true friend will love you even when you've gone astray. Be your son's friend—he's going to need a good one.

We know there is a balance. Fathers can't be their sons' best friend all the time because God has called fathers to lead their sons in a path of godliness, and friction will always arise. However, as I illustrated before, fathers ought not to fall into the other ditch of only correcting, guiding, and calling out because that leads to no relationship at all.

I think a natural question to ask at this point is what does a good friend look like?

Trustworthy

Have you ever felt the sting of someone you thought was trustworthy when they fall through? When this happens, the importance of having trustworthy people in your life seems to be amplified.

People look for people that they can trust, but the process of building trust requires more than just a word of reassurance. The process of building trust is essential in a healthy friendship. The level of trust really determines the depth of friendship. Good friends demonstrate their trustworthiness through the characteristics that I'm going to cover next.

Loyal

One of the greatest demonstrations of trustworthiness is loyalty. It is a kind of faithfulness or steadfastness demonstrated toward someone. Think for a second of someone you really trust. Is that person unpredictable in their support and understanding of you? Hopefully not. We trust people that are faithfully trying to understand us and support us. This is why loyalty is such an important part of building trust and being a good friend. Although, it should be understood that loyalty should be built on a love for the other person and a desire for what's best for them, not built on just trying to please the other person.

Relatable

I need to make a disclaimer with this one. By no means am I telling you, as a father, to start wearing skinny jeans. I'm not telling you to be constantly studied up on the most recent internet fad. What I really want to talk about is this idea of being relatable to your son. Being able to relate to your friend is a big part of friendship. How can a father act as a good friend and relate well with his son? In any relationship, there needs to be authenticity in communicating our experiences, emotions, and thought processes. If the father lacks authenticity in relating his own experiences to his son, his son won't be about to relate to this distorted reality. If a father is going to be a good friend to his son, then there must be authenticity. This requires a certain vulnerability on the father's part. When my father can be real and honest about his own experience in life, it allows me to relate to him in a real and meaningful way. This kind of authentic sharing helps build trust within the relationship.

These are just a few of the things that I believe are important characteristics in a friend, and also good things to strive towards as you become a friend to your son.

I've talked about the tough side of fatherhood—all the tough conversations, guidance, and correction, all the disappointments and struggles. The father-son relationship can be tough, but it is also one of the most beautiful and life-giving mercies that God has given us, even in our fallen world.

Moments Together

When I think of the best moments with my dad, I can't but help think of his laugh. From the time I was a boy, I loved to entertain. I would do anything to get a reaction. From playing characters to doing impressions, I loved to hear people laughing. It's fitting that my name, Isaac, means laughter. I can remember many occasions when my dad and I would sit watching a sporting event and we would be constantly be making jokes at whatever seemed hilarious to us. My dad always seemed to laugh at my jokes, even when they deserved more of a groan. I love to make my dad laugh. I can remember one of my little sisters saying, "Dad, when you laugh, life feels fun!" She was right. Laugh with your son. It may sound trite, but laughter has a way of deepening a relationship in a way that conversation can't.

Intentional action

As I talk about the other side of fatherhood, what I call the friend side, I want to move towards some practical things you can do with your son to build that side of the relationship. I don't want you to see this as an opportunity to compartmentalize your life into the serious and fun side. Life shouldn't be put in boxes like that. I am simply using this wording to highlight the instances of fun and joy, as opposed to the moments of correction and conflict, within the father-son relationship.

That being said, fathers and sons should find things that they both enjoy doing. This may sound like common sense, but I've seen many instances of fathers trying to bond with their sons by doing something they themselves enjoy, rather than things their son enjoys. This usually doesn't go well. When a father goes out of his way to do something fun with his son that the son enjoys, the son feels known, like his father is paying attention to him. He also feels understood, like his father is not only paying attention to where he's at, but that he relates and understands him. If you can have these experiences with your son, even in things that he enjoys, that you may not care for, you are showing him that you are striving intentionally to be with him, understand him, and be his friend. These actions speak to your son louder than any words you could say.

Be intentional about doing things with your son to build the relationship, but as I stated earlier, be mindful of what is most beneficial for him, not just yourself. As a father, you will feel vulnerable as you try to build the friendship intentionally. What if he rejects you? What if he has no desire to be your friend at all? What if you mess up and ruin the small relationship you have now? It feels like a risk that some fathers choose not to take, so the relationship never goes past the do's and don'ts. The son feels disconnected from the father. The father feels disconnected from the son but is too scared of going deeper in the relationship because of the fear of rejection or inadequacy. Many father-son relationships live in this space because both are more comfortable in the kind of relationship with the father giving instructions the son pretending to listen and them both leaving the relationship at that.

As a Christian father, there is a greater calling on your relationship with your son. You ought not just to be his coach, but also his teammate. Coaches instruct, correct, guide, and teach, but you can confide, relate, laugh, and struggle with a teammate. Part of the reason I asked you to be your son's friend is that friends understand you and where you're at. Have you ever had an acquaintance that you felt just didn't understand what you were all about? Those kinds of relationships never go past surface level, because we only like to invite people to our lives that we feel understand us. We let real friends into the most vulnerable places of our lives only when we feel they understand us, then we can move past our worries of rejection. Just like a real friend, a father must establish that ground level of understanding of his son. "I understand you. I'm here to struggle with you. I'm here to laugh with you. I'm not just here to tell you yes or no, I want to have fun with you. I want to be your friend." That is your next step as you continue to journey with your son. Are you his friend or his father? Be both.

LETTER 11:
Courage to Move

Dear Dad,

Do you ever feel like you just don't have it? I mean the "it" that separates the people that do amazing or courageous things and the people like me who don't. What is it that motivates people to perform in front of thousands or run in to save someone stuck in a burning building? What is it that fuels their courage? Sometimes I feel like it's just better for me to stay in the places that I find comfortable. I see some of my friends being courageous in their life, but they seem all in it for themselves. Other guys seem super insecure and don't move to avoid being seen. I'm not sure what to do. How do I live a courageous life? What does that even look like? What should be the motivation of courage? Is it really worth it? I know I've thrown a lot of questions at you, and I don't expect answers now, but I'd love to hear from you.

> Love,
> Your Son

What kind of person lives a courageous life? You may think of a medieval knight stepping into battle or a modern military officer risking his life for his nation, or a doctor helping disease victims in third world countries. All of these people could be good examples of living a courageous life. We, however, have gotten away with the excuse that courage is a personality trait, which some people have and others don't. I remember thinking as a young teen that courage was a special talent that some people had that helped them do amazing things like speaking in front of big crowds or continuing as a missionary even when the financial support is dwindling. We can sometimes put people we think are extraordinarily courageous into a box that we could never reach and rarely have the motivation to strive for. "Those people are different!" We often think that those people are somehow immune to the fear, insecurity, worry, and disappointment in our lives. We think, "I'm not cut out for that kind of courageous life." We make excuses to make ourselves feel better. Because of this, we give sons a pass to live comfortably instead of striving to live courageously. When fathers accept this narrative, they teach their son to strive for comfort more than courage.

Is it possible to live a courageous life where we overcome fear, insecurities, and pride to live out our purpose passionately? A life where our movement is not held back by our laziness but rather propelled forward by our love for God and love for others? Is this kind of life really an option? Is it possible to help your son live courageously too, or is it better to strive for comfort? Let's continue to explore these questions.

Secret Sauce

What holds us back? When I was younger (and even sometimes now), I was obsessed with people at the top of their peer groups who seemed to be at peak performance. Speakers, authors, musicians, athletes—these people went above and beyond what was expected of them and transcended their area of skill. Many of these people didn't have an easy path in life. I don't need to tell you of the many of stories of athletes going from rags to riches. Courage was needed and it wasn't just a one-time decision. It was an act of relentless courage. They seemed to have some kind of special sauce, something that took away all the thoughts of going back, all their fear of failure, all their insecurities, all their worries.

However, that's not true. These people experienced fear, they had insecurities, they had worries, but somehow, either their pride or their hunger for success or hope for a better life or their faith gave them uncomfortable courage. Courage is by nature uncomfortable. The problem is that we make so many excuses not to live courageously that we find it more beneficial to strive for comfort.

Before I go into the areas that I think are important as we seek to live a courageous life, I want to speak about the proper motivations in living courageously.

Growing up playing sports, I noticed one consistent theme in the father-son relationship. I would frequently hear fathers telling their sons to let their pride drive them towards their goal. Now, they wouldn't say it in those terms. They would usually say, "Hey, remember you're the best out there. Don't forget that." On the surface this may seem like harmless encouragement, and perhaps it could be, but I'm still not sure about that. Many of these fathers were teaching their son to let their pride take over and fuel their courage.

Right Fuel = Successful Drive

That brings us to an important question: what should be our fuel for courage? We know it's not a special sauce. Like I said before, some fuel their courage through pride; that is, they allow themselves to get out of their comfort zone and be courageous because they are driven by their pride. Pride is a powerful thing. It can help men achieve amazing feats, goals thought to be unreachable, success thought to be unachievable. However, that does not mean pride is good. When it is used as courage fuel, it is by nature selfish. This kind of selfish courage is only a means to more self-advancement. However, in our culture, where the definition of success is defined by your bank account, the fame you've achieved, and the respect you are given, this kind of prideful fuel is seen as a good thing. But is it? Is pride really a good fuel for living a courageous life?

Others let fear fuel their courage. Fear is a powerful fuel too. Some let the fear of failure hold them back from living a courageous life, but others let fear of insignificance drive them to do things that few would have the courage to do. This fear of insignificance hits us in the very core of our being. We want to be known and valued, yet we fear those desires will never be fulfilled. This fear drives many people into doing courageous things, that without fear, they would have never done in the first place.

We see the people who on the surface seem to be living courageous life, but after a closer look they seem to be ether fueled by pride or by their fear of insignificance, or a combination of the two. We ask, is courage motivated by selfishness really the key to living a courageous life? Don't think of this as an insignificant question. Your son is exploring the different fuels for his courage. He may have friends who see pride as the best fuel for their courage and ultimate success. Perhaps he is using his fear of insignificance to drive him to get out of his comfort zone. He is looking for the right fuel. Which one will sustain him as he lives a courageous life? He's not sure. I wasn't sure. I loved to look at the most successful people and see what took them to the top of their craft, most often what I say was an astounding level of self-confidence (not a healthy level) or almost a childish fear of being rendered insignificant.

What kind of fuel should you encourage your son to thrive on? What kind of fuel should you use to drive your courage as you model a courageous life for your son? These questions may seem to have many answers, but as Christians, I want to suggest two ideas that ought to be the fuel of our courage. First, our love for God. Second, our love for others.

Courage should only be admired when used to fulfill a good goal. Courage for a selfish end is not to be commended. When courage is only a means to fulfilling our love of self, then we miss God's true call on us to live a courageous life. Earlier, I talked about encouraging your son to live for God and to live for a greater purpose than the one the culture is telling him to embrace. As we think about living a courageous life, we need to understand for whom we are living this courageous life. Courage can be a powerful tool to get where we want in life, but that does not mean that is what we should use it for—namely, a selfish goal. We ought to live this life with a courage that is fueled by our love for God. But why love God? This sounds like an obvious answer for a Christian, and hopefully, it is for you, but I don't want you to assume that it is for your son. I can't stress this enough: don't assume your son has an answer. Sometimes Christian fathers become so caught up in telling their sons to love God, they forget to tell them why! It's not hard to answer the question of why to love God, I could write another book just dedicated to that, but it is important that you not assume that your son knows the answer. Tell him.

Our courage needs to be filled by a love for God and for others. What does that look like? I want to highlight three areas as we think about living a courageous life. Through covering those topics, hopefully you can begin to see why the fuel of our courage is so important and why courage is a necessity in these aspects of life.

A Letter to My Father

Where Does He Stand?

At the beginning of the chapter, I talked about what a courageous life could look like. Warriors, soldiers, firefighters, and missionary doctors are prime examples of people demonstrating courage. However, for us, the fathers and young men who seem to have "normal" lives, what does a courageous life look like? What does it look like for you? What does it look like for your son?

One of my goals of this book is for you to help your son build his vision for living a courageous life for God. However, that can only begin when you can start an ongoing conversation on what a courageous life looks like and what demonstrating courage within his own life could look like today. Ask your son probing questions on what he sees as a courageous life. By doing this, you'll began to get a glimpse of where your son stands on this idea of living courageously.

It can be easy to be overwhelmed when you try to help your son do something that you still have trouble with. "How am I supposed to help my son live a courageous life when I'm not even sure if I am living one?" That is the right question to ask, but we ought not to leave it unanswered as an excuse to give up. Remember, God's not asking you to be a perfect father, He's asking you to be a courageous father. But wait, you thought all this courage stuff was for your son. Nope, it's for you too. If you are going to begin to change your life based on what I have said in this book, you are going to need tremendous courage. You're not a perfect example, and that's okay, but it's not okay to use that as an excuse. Don't give up. Let today be the beginning of yours and your son's journey into a courageous life. Now, we see what that looks like.

Courage in Relationships

The idea of having courage in a relationship may be one of the last qualities you think to be relevant. We think of love, patience, and humility being important in relationships. So where does courage come in? In fact, all of those qualities take courage. It takes great courage to love unconditionally. I can remember times when my dad would differ to my mom even when it was difficult for him. I saw the courage it took him. He showed love even when it was difficult. It takes courage. But courage fueled by pride will never choose to love even when it's tough. In those times, my dad's courage was fueled by a love for God and a love for my mom.

Too many people don't understand the idea of having courage in relationships. They think relationships should be easy, completely fulfilling, fun, and comfortable, when in fact God-glorifying relationships are marked by the courage in them. As a father, let your relationships be marked by the courage you display in them. When your son sees you being courageous in your relationship with him, you are providing him with a living picture of what a God-glorifying relationship looks like. He needs to see that in you. Courage, not perfection.

Courage in Convictions

Christians believe many things that the culture around us thinks are stupid. We have convictions that make us seem weird to others. We live differently, or at least we should. This makes us stand out, maybe not intentionally, but it does whether we like it or not. One of my greatest weaknesses is trying to make everyone like me. When I was younger, I passed on opportunities to speak the truth and instead, I conformed to what I thought others wanted. I didn't have the courage to stand on my convictions. In this case, it wasn't that I had the wrong fuel for my courage, but that I chose conformity instead of having my love for God and others fuel my courage to stand on my convictions. Men, whether young or old, are constantly confronted with a decision to choose conformity to maintain comfort or to choose courage to stand on our convictions.

During the early stages of my parent's marriage, they decided that when they had kids, they wanted to homeschool us. It was their conviction that God wanted them to homeschool, no matter how strange or looked down upon it might have been. It was their conviction, despite the possible discomfort that could follow. It is hard to stick to your conviction even when others see them as strange or wrong. That is when real courage is needed. Young men need to see more of this courage. When we do, it challenges us to have the same courage in our convictions.

As Christian, we have convictions in what we believe about God, and in what we will and will not do. Your son is going to run into people that will not believe what he believes. They may mock and laugh at him. Will your son have the courage to stand for his convictions?

Entering university was a real and tangible opportunity to stand firmly on my conviction of Christian faith. However, one time I chose to conform to fit in with other students. I thought it was no big deal—a compromise here and there wouldn't hurt—but I was actually making an important decision. I needed to listen to my love for God instead of my fear of not fitting in and let that fuel my courage in standing on my convictions. Your son needs the right fuel for his courage, and he needs to let his love for God overcome his fear of man.

In chapter 9, I talked about the issues of purity and marriage. It is my hope that you would help your son develop strong convictions regarding his sexual purity. It is so important for young men to start developing these convictions from an early age.

What are your son's convictions? Will he have the courage to stand for them? We would like to think that we have the courage to stand on our own. We would like to think that we're stronger than we actually are. All of us, fathers and sons, we must rely on God for a renewed fuel. Part of living a courageous life is relying on God for a renewed fuel for our courage. If fathers and sons try to stand on their conviction alone, they will be worn out and word down. We need each other. Our fuel for our courage can only be sustained by God. Alone we will grow weary, but living a courageous life is about the long haul, not just the here and now. Whether it is courage in relationships or courage in standing for our convictions, we not only need to be using the right fuel, but we must continually ask God to refuel us. Will your son be able to stand courageously for his convictions? Tell him who supplies the fuel for our courage. That is where he'll find the courage in the midst of fear. Let's unpack that.

The Courage to Move

I've mentioned before that as a teenager and pre-teen, I struggled with anxiety. Anxiety, fear, and insecurities drive so many young men into a state of hopelessness. How can we ever live a courageous and fulfilling life for God if we are overwhelmed with our fears, worries, and insecurities at every corner? Is it really worth it? What makes courage worth it? You son asks himself this question every time he is given the opportunity to move courageously, whether in regard to convictions, relationships, or anywhere in between. Because being courageous comes at a cost. When we chose to act courageously, something is given up. Whatever it may be, it usually comes back to comfort. We ask ourselves, "Is courage worth the loss of earthly comfort?" Others would consider the material or social benefits of courage. At first glance, this may seem like a reasonable method, but when we think this way, we are forgetting the motivation of our courage. It should be to follow Jesus and grow more like Him and closer to Him each day. That is the fuel of our courage. It is fueled by God, refueled through God, and revealed for God! This is a missing piece of the puzzle for so many sons. They ask, is it worth it? Your son needs to hear from their father that not only is courage worth the loss of comfort, but it will change their life when we step out from their comfort and live courageously through God, and for God. That changes everything. Your son needs to hear that. Take courage and lead him towards a courageous life.

LETTER 12:
Looking for Success, Finding Wisdom

Dear Dad,

Over these past couple of weeks, I've been thinking a lot about my goals. It's sometimes difficult for me to decide what I should be striving for. I see my friends and some are trying to get into the big schools so they can get the high paying job that will provide them with the life they dreamed of. I see others striving for fame, who try to get people's attention and build their lives around that influence. Still others seem unmotivated and are complacent, with no real-life goals at all. I want to be successful, but I don't know what is most important in life. I figure you might be able to help. What should I be reaching for, and how do I get there?

Love,
Your Son.

What are you striving for? If God could grant one request that you would ask of him for yourself, what would it be? Most would say some kind of success: success in your relationships, career, or spiritual life. The list goes on. "I want to be rich" or "I want to be powerful" are some of the most common answers for young men. Sometimes young men like to think that all aspects of their lives should converge to reach one destination. We take a moment to think about what's at that destination. Money, fame, notoriety, power, authority. We hope that the destination will bring us something greater, happiness, meaning, or acceptance. You may say that Christian young men never think this way, but you would be mistaken. Even young men that have given their lives to Christ by repenting and trusting in Jesus still have the stain of distorted thinking on their lives. There can be a disconnection. There was for me.

The years of later adolescence are interesting. We are told to work hard, make the right decisions, and choose the right interests so that we might succeed passed high school. We are forced, perhaps for the first time, to look at what we want our life to be and what goals we want to pursue. For me, even as a Christian, I saw being wealthy as a desirable goal. However, it wasn't about the money for me. I wanted people to look at me and say, "What an awesome guy." Looking back now, it sounds funny, but it wasn't to me then. I was reaching after financial success so people would not only respect me but that they would like me. In my mind, I was willing to compromise not pursuing a career that I may have liked for the trade off of looking successful.

Too often, many young men are caught up in this chase for success. However, this isn't only young men's problem. Many men choose success over other parts of their lives. I feel our priorities as men have been in the wrong place. I want to help you guide your son toward something more important than success. To help me do this, I want us to dig into the story of a guy named Solomon.

Solomon wasn't just a regular guy, he was a king! The king of Israel. We find this story in 1 Kings, chapter 1. Solomon loved God. He had seen the example that his father, King David, and wanted to continue this legacy of faithfulness to God. During Solomon's reign, God met him in a dream and posed him with the same question that I asked you earlier. Ask one thing of God and it will be done. What did Solomon ask? That his nation would become a giant empire? That he would be the wealthiest person in all the world? One would think that his request would be something rare and tangible, material perhaps, but Solomon was aware of what was most important. He could have asked for riches or military success, but instead he asked for wisdom. Why would he do that? When we try to think of what will make us most effective in serving God on this earth, we may think of resources like money and popularity. In fact, the greatest key to our effectiveness as a Christian in serving God is wisdom.

What is most important? What should I spend my time on? What career should I pursue? What person should I marry? What opportunities should I take? Which ones are a waste of time? Your son has questions so foundational that they impact his very existence, but others so small that they could be brushed off with a laugh. In both, he desires answers. David wasn't able to answer all of Solomon's questions. He wasn't able to help him make all of his decisions. What David could do was to help him develop a hunger for wisdom. Have you read the psalms? They are packed full of God's wisdom written down by David. We must conclude that David possessed a hunger for God's wisdom, a love that he passed down to his son. When Solomon was given the ability to request something from God, he chose wisdom. It wasn't a fluke request; he had seen how the driving force of Godly wisdom had characterized much of his father life. But we think of our own lives, would we choose wisdom? Do we choose wisdom? Does your son choose wisdom? Or is he running after something else?

Give Me This One Thing

We all have had a desire to receive something from God, some more important than others. When we pray, we ask, but what for? You could be asking God to break a cycle of sin, to heal a sick friend, to save a rebellious teen, to give you joy, to give you peace, but how about to give you success? Success in sharing the gospel, sure. Success in serving our community better, of course. But perhaps one of our requests, from fathers and sons, which is rarely verbalized, is for personal success. We all want to get ahead in the game and a little (preferably big) nudge in a successful direction couldn't hurt.

Back when I played basketball, there would be times in practice that I would daydream about scoring fifty points. This was community league so if a team's score got to fifty, they had a good shooting day. I thought of all the people that would be amazed, I thought of the legend I would become. My teammates would never stop talking about it. I asked, "God, could you just help me do this, just once?" I didn't want to overstep, I thought that one God-given spectacular basketball game wasn't too much to ask, but at the same time, I knew it wasn't going to happen. God wasn't just going to help me have an awe-inspiring basketball performance just because that was what I wanted. However, it does show me a glimpse of my heart's desire then, and the desires I still battle now. I wanted to succeed. More important, I wanted other people to see me as successful. That desire was a driving force for much of my teen years.

Please note that I'm not saying that wisdom and financial or relational success or gaining recognition are mutually exclusive. However, for your son, I want you to help encourage him towards wisdom with the possibility of that outward success, not striving for success at all cost, and throwing wisdom aside.

You see this tendency with young men. They see a way to make a quick buck or gain popularity and they pursue it without much discernment. Part of striving for wisdom ahead of success is thinking long term. So often as young man, we let our short-sighted perspective govern how we behave, but part of being wise is being able to take look to the future and make decisions that are not just for the here and now. Sons need wisdom to be able to take on a big picture perspective.

I want you to get in the mindset of your son. As he's getting older, he feels the pressure of the world to make money, to get married, to gain recognition, to be successful. Your son thinks, "If only I were successful…" As you're trying to get in the mind of your son, or even yourself when you were his age, success can seem like the fix-all. That is, as long as I'm successful, whether financially, relationally, or in status, my life will go well. The temptation to put his striving for success above everything else is real. The voice of the culture around him that tells him that success is most important is loud. However, when we look back at Solomon, we see that God was pleased with his request for wisdom. This is important for us to understand today. Even though Solomon could have requested to be successful in ways that may have helped him serve God, God desired Solomon to choose something more powerful and important than success.

For your son, the idea that wisdom is more important than success may be a 180-degree change in thinking. For so many young men, we see success as a remedy to our insecurities, fear, lack of clarity in life, and so on. We think that somehow if success can be obtained, we will be okay. Wisdom, however, doesn't seem to promise any such things. Discernment, an important aspect of wisdom, is not something that young men usually find valuable. But as you know, the value of wisdom cannot be understated. Okay, if God wants your son to pursue wisdom above his search for success, then how can you encourage him in that when the world is telling him the opposite?

Think back to Solomon. He saw how wisdom had played a major role in his father David's life, whether in his military decisions, his role as king, or his faithfulness to God throughout his life. Solomon saw it all. Sons naturally imitate their fathers. Yes, the stain of sin has affected and distorted the father-son relationship; sons do rebel and fathers can be bad examples. Regardless, this imitation still happens. A son will see his father yearning for wisdom, or see him overtaken by his impulsivity. Let him see your hunger for wisdom by your openness to correction, and by striving to learn. Not only should you be striving for these things, but you want your son to as well. In this next section, I'll talk more about the key aspects of wisdom.

Roadblock

Does your son think he needs your advice, guidance, and correction? This is an important question to ask as we talk about wisdom. To be hungry for wisdom, as you want your son to be, he needs to believe that he doesn't have all of it. It's like trying to get someone to search for food even though they've deceived themselves into thinking they are full. I don't know if you've noticed, but young men can be stubborn. Wouldn't you be stubborn if you were always right? Of course you would be, but you know you are not, and your son is definitely not. However, he may not know that, or perhaps he knows but acts as if he is always right. This is not just ignorance, it is pride. God calls young men to humility. Without it, your son will never hunger for wisdom and seek it out. This is a huge issue for most young men.

You can fall into two ditches on this issue as a father. The first is focusing too much on your son's shortcomings; that is, where your son is lacking, either in knowledge, insight, or character. When fathers fall into this ditch, their sons start to internalize that feeling of inadequacy. However, they are keenly aware of what they do not know but are less likely to be confident in what they actually know.

The other ditch is when they focus too much on commending what their son knows. Sometimes in this ditch, their sons model their fathers, in which they only focus on what they do know but have no interest in finding out what they don't know, and further, not seeking out wisdom. I want you to notice that I have not told you that you should never point out the weaknesses in your son or that you should never commend him for what he knows. However, there has been a turn in the last decade for fathers to be good at encouraging and commending their sons in what they do know, but paying little attention on what their sons don't know. I think this plays into the epidemic of "know-it-all" young men, but I don't want to place the blame primarily on fathers.

There is another factor at work: your son's heart. It is pulled toward pride and stubbornness. For your son to begin to hunger after wisdom, he must rid himself of the dilution that he is already full. He needs a heart change. It can be easy as a father to get angry and frustrated with your son when he's acting as though he knows everything. I urge you not to throw in the towel. God is working. Don't remove yourself from that work in your son's life. Sometimes, it takes a young man moving to a new and perhaps stretching season, which will humble him. Regardless of the circumstances around these heart changes, remember that his pride won't be broken by you talking down to him or moving into the other ditch of only criticizing and correcting. Even if he is humbled by that, by doing it that way you are also giving him an incorrect view of God's perspective of him. You are telling him that he is a failure, not in a moral sense, but in a personhood sense. This is not a helpful or effective shortcut in trying to change your son's heart. If you're only trying to enact a behavioral response from your son, you are missing the mark. You need to point him to God's perspective. Then he can understand that wisdom is a gift from God and should be pursued. Pride and this "know it all" tendencies are inconsistent with biblical thinking.

At the end of the day, only God can establish a hunger for wisdom in your son, but just like David did for Solomon, you can help inspire him towards that way of thinking. Are you open to correction? Do you seek out other people when you don't know something? If you don't seek out wisdom, your son will see no reason to pursue it. However, by modeling that kind of humble character, you will help point your son towards his own journey of seeking wisdom.

There was a reason that I left the topic of wisdom to near the end, because as you leave this book, hopefully better equipped to begin a deeper relationship with your son, I want you to guide your son towards wisdom and seek God's wisdom for yourself. That's where the game is changed. As much as you may want to help your son, only God's wisdom will begin to affect your father-son relationship in a powerful way. This is our springboard for the last chapter, when we jump into where to go with your son after reading this book. This is going to be a game changer.

LETTER 13:
Where do we go from here?

Dear Dad,

In writing these letters, I thought about stopping many times. I just about gave up this relationship, but I've kept writing. I've told you so many things that lay heavy on my heart, questions that surround my mind, longings of my soul. I want to be real and honest with you. So today, I want to ask you one more question for now. Are you ready to write back? I'll be waiting here when you are.

Love,
Your Son

There are defining moments in each one of our lives. Decisions we make, the guidance we apply, and actions we follow through with all play into our unraveling story. Our story, however, is not left in isolation. It affects others in a tangible way. We are not merely bystanders in other's lives, but we are participants. For parents, this becomes a reality when they are given the responsibility to care for a child. In the beginning, there was no option to be a bystander. With so many needs, participating in this child's story was not merely an option, but your God-given calling. Rambunctious but kind, if your eyes left him for too long, you feared he would get into something. As the father, you hope you are doing it right, reading the right books, listening to the right parenting seminars, going to the right conferences, putting good influences around him, hoping that this will get him on the right path towards a Godly and fulfilling life. As he gets into his teen years, a distance begins to form, and this gap seems to get wider as the years pass. The reason? You're not exactly sure. You figure, he's older now, he needs his space, he needs to spend time with his friends. You know he has a pretty good head on his shoulders and you believe he'll figure it out. Those points make sense to you, for the most part. He needs space, of course, but you know it's more than that. You feel like you are no longer a participant in his story, but rather a bystander. You get frustrated and feel inadequate. You want to be intentional, but all the books and advice your given seem to skim over the complexities of relationships. Your son, meanwhile, sees this gap in the relationship getting wider. He assumes it's just natural. "Dad did his part, now I have to figure it out." Sure, it would be nice to be able to talk to his dad about important topics and answer questions that his friends seem to have no grasp of, but this must be the way it goes, he thinks. This all too often characterizes the modern father-son relationship. Fathers feel either apathetic or ill equipped to deepen their relationship and to act as a mentor to their son. Sons lean into their independence but lack the wisdom to ask for guidance. We are left at a standstill.

Maybe you picked up this book to help you bridge the relational gap between you and your son. You have read with expectations of what you thought I would say through the lens of what you've already heard or read. As you near the end of the book, I hope you feel encouraged to become a participant in your son's life and make a real, lasting impact. I also hope you have been challenged to once again walk in the shoes of a young man and better understand your son.

However, as much as I want to congratulate you on finishing this book, this is not the end. We think about doing hundreds of things, we talk about doing tons of things, but we only really do a couple. What sets those things apart? Why is it that you said you were going to lose weight, yet you bailed on the diet the second week? Why is it that you said you would make more time for reading your Bible, yet it keeps getting pushed to the side? What is it to say that even after you read this whole book about re-establishing and deepening your relationship with your son, yet at the first sign of difficulty you'll want to through in the towel?

You are at a crossroad. You've made a good first step. Too many fathers see this distance between their sons as inevitable. Too many sons see this gap forming in their relationships with their father as natural. Because of this, there is no intentional moment to prevent this all too common reality. Thankfully, you didn't buy into this lie or at least are seeing the truth now.

The truth is that it is a lot harder to build a strong father-son relationship then we'd like to think. We would hope everything fell into our lap. Parenting is hard enough for a father and navigating the adolescent and teen years is hard enough for a son. But yet, we need to realize this stuff takes real work. Even after reading this book, you still may not feel ready. Thoughts of inadequacy creep in. Fear of failing as a father can hold a powerful grip on you. You ask yourself, where do I go from here?

First

Go to Christ. Only through his power and presence in every area of your life will He begin to help you bridge this looming relational gap between you and your son. The Holy Spirit needs to play an important role in you and your son's journey together. All of the principles that I urged you to enact with your son can only be demonstrated with Christ working through you. He will give you words. He will give you courage. He will give you wisdom. Only when you understand that your performance as a father is not a one-man show will the pressure that you feel on your shoulders to get everything right be lifted. It's not a one-man show. You're not always going to say the right thing. You're not always going to give perfect guidance. However, when you are working according to God's calling on your life, that is to be an important part of your son's life, you can be at peace. Regardless of the struggle and difficulty that may arise, God will provide you with everything necessary to fulfill your calling as a father. God will never fail you.

Second

Go to your son. This is going to look different for each father. It may start with an apology and a chance to start over. For others, this may just be a chance to become more intentional in your relationship with your son. Still others are fighting an uphill battle: your son has turned the other way, wants nothing to do with you, and your relationship seems to be gasping for air. Regardless of which one of these you identify with the most, my encouragement to you is simple: Be there. Let him see you there. Yes, communication is key, but your presence with him is the beginning point as you bridge the distance that has started to form or has resided over you both for too long.

We can look at our heavenly father, the perfect father, and seek to grasp at just a few aspects of His nature. His presence, He is with us. Our Father is with us. When Christians can perceive God's presence through their day, throughout the struggles, the successes, and the headaches, they can still overflow with peace. They sense that God is with them, and with that comes a sense of comfort, reassurance, understanding, and power that comes from God. This is life changing.

When a father is with his son—not only in person, but when he can sense his own father's approval, understanding, and reassurance—his son feels a sense of peace. That is the beginning of real trust to take place and open the lines of communication. You make a powerful statement about God to your son when you are there for him when you are faithfully present in his life, he can grasp the fact that God is always present within our lives. Show him Christ through your presence but acknowledge when you've been absent in his life. The last thing I want happening when a father reads this book is to tell his son to sit down and precede to smash open his life with a proverbial sledgehammer and try to start giving advice and guidance and expecting him to open up to you. You'll only do more damage. Trust needs to be your relational foundation. Trust takes time but your son is worth taking the time to build his trust.

Though a gap is present in many father-son relationships, this doesn't change the reality that sons need their fathers desperately—for correction, for direction, for wisdom, for acceptance, for love. Sons need their fathers to be real with them, to be able to have an authentic relationship with them. This is essential. A real relationship between a father and his son where he can tell his son the things he needs to hear, "I love you. I'm proud of you. I'm on your side." They need a real and authentic relationship where a father can point him to something greater, someone greater. This is a loving relationship where sons can come forward with their questions and doubt and are not ignored, but encouraged to seek out what really matters in life. It's a relationship where even through trial, a father can wait for his son to come home. Each can spur the other on towards living a courageous life for Christ, and fathers value their son's quest for wisdom rather than temporal success. Both fathers and sons need this kind of relationship. It will not come easy. God will use this journey to transform both fathers and their sons. It will be painful, but it will be worth it.

Closing Thoughts

While writing this book, there were moments when I looked back on my manuscript and asked some questions. I wondered what would actually result from the project. Would father and son relationships be restored? Will fathers better understand their sons? Will sons better understand their fathers? Will this book be picked up, skimmed through, and left on a bookshelf with others that had been read yet forgotten? Would this book actually encourage fathers and sons to be intentional about their relationships? Maybe. I hope so. This is my prayer. But at the end of the day, it's not about this book, it's about a real, authentic relationship that needs to take place for the good of both of you. This is what God has called you to. Don't run from God any longer. It's time that you join the journey. This is your turning point!

> *"And He will turn the hearts of fathers to their children and the hearts of children to their fathers,"*
>
> Malachi 4:6a

About the Author

Isaac Mogilevsky is a writer, filmmaker, speaker, and founder/director of Daily Disciple Ministry and dailydisciple.ca. He has a passion for helping people become authentic, inspired, and passionate disciples of Jesus. In 2016, as a teenager, while being home educated he founded Daily Disciple Ministry, publishing weekly articles online from a Biblical worldview. Today, through Daily Disciple Ministry, thousands of the ministry's online followers receive weekly videos, articles, and other resources to help them grow as disciples of Jesus. Isaac currently resides in Winnipeg, Manitoba. For more information and to watch the short film made in tandem with this book, please visit: alettertomyfather.ca.

Printed in Canada